Fighting Myself

Ian McCranor

MAPLE
PUBLISHERS

Fighting With Myself

Author: Ian McCranor

Copyright © Ian McCranor (2023)

The right of Ian McCranor to be identified as author of this work has been asserted by the author in accordance with section 77 and 78 of the Copyright, Designs and Patents Act 1988.

First Published in 2023

ISBN 978-1-915796-78-3 (Paperback)
      978-1-915996-58-9 (E-Book)

Book cover and Book layout by:

    White Magic Studios
    www.whitemagicstudios.co.uk

Published by:

    Maple Publishers
    Fairbourne Drive, Atterbury,
    Milton Keynes,
    MK10 9RG, UK
    www.maplepublishers.com

A CIP catalogue record for this title is available from the British Library.

Contents

Introduction

This book isn't just about me or my violent encounters. As you continue reading you'll realise this book is actually about you - the 'you' who at times has found yourself scared of the world and have wondered how your life is relevant within it. The 'you' who has felt unworthy and struggled with your self-esteem, the 'you' who has little confidence and find it so much easier to just live in the shadows and experience life as a spectator. I was 'you' until I proclaimed I am not going to allow this any longer. I stopped being 'you' when I said 'I am' going to be confident and 'I am' going to be someone.

There have been plenty of books written by hard men, fighters who have shared stories about a life engulfed with violence and crime. Through their writings some tried to convince you that the violence they encountered was not of their making that they were just normal people living normal lives and somehow violence came looking for them. They were telling you all this while at the same time harbouring anger over being wronged and their training regime being fuelled by revenge. They asked you to believe that you could do what they had done, become strong and confident and by simply following their example you could be just like them.

What they failed to address however was that you, like most people, could never really be like them because you are simply not built that way. I am not built that way either but I had discovered that it didn't matter; I didn't have to become a hard-man to gain respect, I didn't have to fight with anyone and everyone to build a reputation.

As you continue to read, you will come across the word Karate mentioned many times, so I would like to take this opportunity to explain exactly what karate really is, or should I say, what it means to me at least. Karate is many things to many people so the definition you get will depend on the person you are talking to.

Karate was my initial 'go to' activity that gave me a purpose, something that had me setting goals for myself and ultimately turned me into an athlete who went on to compete in a combat sport. That's it, that's all it was, but like I said, if you were to ask another practitioner they would most probably give you a totally different answer.

I have absolutely no doubt that whoever you are and whatever life you lead, you will see yourself in so many of these pages. This was a very difficult book for me to write as it asked me to open up about so many things that I had chosen to either ignore or just plain old hide. Most of the people who knew me in my younger years only knew the "me" that I'd chosen to show them, because just like so many people, I often didn't think the real me was good enough.

Chapter #1

The Bouncer

Blood poured from his nose and mouth making the extent of the damage difficult to comprehend. I knew his jaw was broken, I'd felt it dislocate and heard that familiar bone-on-bone sound. His head had been pushed up against the wall with nowhere else to go. I took a small step back to fire a combination of kicks and punches all of which hit their mark. Now he lay unconscious in the doorway, still clutching the broken bottle which was intended for my face.

I am a bouncer. I'll say that once again - I am a bouncer. 'I am' are the most powerful words you can ever say aloud, and, followed with an absolute intention, is how affirmation manifests itself. It's how I became the person I wanted to be. I never wanted to be a bouncer though, but it was a means by which I became the strong, confident man that I'd always desired to be. The man I am today is the result of having to deal with and confront my lack of confidence and it was this lack of confidence that was steering my decision-making on a daily basis. The decisions that I'm referring to are the ones made in our youth that will ultimately shape our future. My future, had I not taken these steps, was destined to be one that would have seen me permanently cowering under the weight of fear.

As a bouncer I was a hard fucker and still, to this day, refuse to be someone who can be bullied or taken advantage of. I'm also a very compassionate and caring man, a fiercely loyal person who isn't afraid when the going gets tough. Throughout my journey of becoming a bouncer, a bouncer who didn't shy away or run when the chips were down, I quickly discovered that 'I am' became my friend - nurturing a new mindset, new actions and new behaviours. Until then I used 'I am' mostly to reinforce negative manifestations such as 'I am not good enough', 'I am going to lose', 'I am shy' or 'I am scared'. Telling myself these things as a young child had influenced the young man I was becoming. I had no idea that telling myself these things was ultimately ordering my fate. I had sat in life's restaurant picking negativity from the menu and then I was disappointed when my order was served up in abundance, along with a side of self-pity.

It was a Saturday night in a once thriving industrial city. The 1970's and 1980's in Coventry saw high unemployment after the collapse of British motorcycle production, and later, the motor industry. The cathedral ruins in the heart of Coventry were a stark and haunting reminder of the relentless air raids of November 1940, courtesy of Hitler's boys during the Second World War. This was only a stone's throw from a hugely popular pub/nightclub in the early 1990's. The Dog and Trumpet, affectionately known as The Dog, was primarily a student, alternative-scene venue but Saturday nights at the Dog welcomed all comers. In those days once the club was full the main doors were closed. After pubs closed punters would generally make their way to their nightclub of choice and stay there until closing time unlike today's drinkers who drift from one venue to another, owing to the late licence drinking culture. Once the front doors of The Dog were closed the only way in or out was via a long and sloping passageway to the rear, leading to security doors which brought you to the concrete spiral that was the Barracks' car park. Nobody was allowed to loiter in the passageway except for the staff but given that this area was quiet and relatively cooler, handfuls of people would make their way here to escape the hustle and bustle or just cool off, especially those feeling a bit worse for wear. A blind eye was turned as long as no one took the piss.

The bouncers would often stand at the top of the passageway to take advantage of the quiet space and chat. From here we could still see pretty much most of the floor area so it was a great spot to escape the crowds whilst keeping a watchful eye on things. Most evenings you would find me walking around amongst the clubbers, mixing and chatting with the crowd. Being a bouncer isn't just about stopping people coming in, breaking up fights and chatting up women (although all of these are included in the job description); spotting and stopping trouble before it starts is a massive part of the job and to be able to do this you need to be on the ball and be able to de-escalate a situation before a full-blown kick-off begins.

This particular Saturday night was like any other. I'd been walking around the standing area of the club when I noticed a commotion at the bar around 20 feet away involving one of the bar staff. I made my way through the crowd and was soon in the thick of it trying to quickly understand what was going on. At the very least it was an argument between the barmaid and two lads over one of them being short-changed but it had escalated into insults and threats. One lad was insistent that he'd handed over a twenty-pound note but the barmaid was adamant it was a tenner. Stalemate. Waiting for the till to be cashed up at the end of the night was the only solution, but the lad didn't want to wait that long, and the situation grew more tense. As it happened, I had chatted to both lads on a previous night, not on a personal level but I'd seen them in the club many times. Both were decent lads who had never been involved in any trouble, but I also knew the barmaid was trustworthy and it was most likely just a mistake. I made a suggestion. I reached into my pocket and pulled out a tenner, offering it to the lad. I told him I would either get my money back from the till when it was cashed up, or if not, he'd owe it to me. He looked a bit worried and made it clear that even though he was 100% sure that he was correct, he also didn't want me looking for him next time he was in town. "Well," I said, "it's your call. You can take the cash or wait 'til 3am." He took the money; I got my tenner back later when the till was actually up.

A short while later I was doing my usual circuit through the crowds when I was approached by a lad and his girlfriend who warned me that a group of people on the raised area were tipping drinks over those below them and generally causing trouble. I made my way over to check it out. By now the place was rammed, getting over to where these guys were would take a while. One of the glass collectors collared me, "It's about to kick off over there, some wanker just threw a drink over me and he just slapped some bird." I pretty much recall exactly what he said because I remember thinking, 'slapped some bird? Who the fuck talks like that?!' With each step towards the situation, which I could now see rumbling in the crowd ahead of me, it was becoming more obvious that this wasn't going to be resolved with just a little chat. People were starting to distance themselves from the area and as they did so I could hear mumbles predicting the outcome. I asked someone to tell the DJ to get on the mic to ask for more doormen but no sooner had I finished speaking I realised I was only feet away from three pissed up bullies who looked like they didn't give a flying fuck about anything. Everyone knows the type - cocky, arrogant and most likely fuelled by a line of coke, a combination that convinced them they were invincible. This is something that most people don't understand about the job of a bouncer, it isn't just dealing with normal, rational people who will respond to a quiet chat about their behaviour. Quite often, like in this situation, I wasn't going to be dealing with just a person. I was going to be dealing with a behaviour that was being controlled by whatever substances had been ingested.

As I approached them on the raised area I quickly realised that any effort towards meaningful and calm conversation would be futile. They were in full swing, sabotaging the night out of those standing around them. My mind quickly turned to which of them I would need to destroy first. Every experienced doorman will tell you that although talking someone down off the ledge is the ideal and preferable approach, the presence of drugs or alcohol, sometimes both, means there is simply no hope for a non-violent resolution. All three lads were now trading insults with a few girls who instead of wisely leaving the area had decided to hang around and throw fuel onto a fire which, by the second, was spiralling more and more out of control, and just to add to the tension I was now being egged on to throw them out by the infuriated bystanders. Hearing all of this, the lads who had now seen me approaching turned their full attention to me with the all too familiar stance which screamed, 'If I'm leaving, you'd better fucking well make me.' One of the lads was cockily leaning against a horizontal wooden handrail that ran the length of the raised platform that we all stood on. He gave me that all-familiar head nod that screamed 'Now, what the fuck are you gonna do about it?' With both of his hands tucked neatly into his front pockets he looked straight at me and mumbled something that I couldn't hear above the music but I didn't need to hear anything, his body language was loud and clear! He nudged his mate who was stood to his right-hand side and they both nodded back at me and smiled, chuckling to themselves. The sidekick leaned in to say something in his ear, their two heads bumped together. These two were now holding each other up, spilling beer as they laughed deliriously. There was no mistake these lads were there for violence, they may have been drunk but they knew exactly what they were doing.

I started scanning my surroundings, realising that no other doorman had yet turned up, and I'd not even heard the DJ put out the call to arms. I was on my own for now. My heart was racing and my mouth was getting drier by the second - Mother Nature once again doing her thing. I'd been here so many times before but each time is different and never loses any of its impact, each instance just makes you feel sick to the stomach. As I moved closer and positioned myself for the inevitable I spotted weapons in the guise of bottles and beer mugs everywhere. This needed to be quick and it needed to be brutal. It was obvious now what they were up to and I'd found myself smack bang in the middle of it. The hardest part of any altercation is the moments just before and just after, the altercation itself is what you train for, or at least it should be, but there's no real training for the pre-fight and post-fight emotions. These are the moments that fuck your head up. I was now in pre-fight mode and I needed to get into position.

As a doorman I had a tried and tested method of getting physically close to potential aggressors whilst not making them too alarmed. Using the 'I'm clueless and ignorant to what's going on' approach I kept these lads in my line of vision. I then focused on the crowd behind them and made reference to what someone else was doing, asking an imaginary bystander behind them to get off the table. The ploy worked and the lads were momentarily distracted and disarmed, handing me just the window of opportunity I needed. Boom! My forehead crashed into the face of the 'hands-in-pockets' lad sending him backwards and almost over the guardrail followed by a sharp right cross landing cleanly on the jaw of number two. He was out cold the second it landed. Number three looked on stunned, scared and thought better of getting involved, but it was too late to change my mind now. He raised his hands, "OK, OK, stop, stop." I grabbed the front of his jacket with both hands and pulled his face onto my forehead. The thud was sickening and was heard amongst the bystanders as the music fell silent like some saloon bar brawl in the old westerns. Hands-in-pockets guy, who was still upright but with no fight left in him, appeared right in front of me but a short, left hook put him on the floor next to his mate. All three were now out cold. By now my fellow bouncers had arrived and we all proceeded to haul the three down the passageway to be kicked out the back doors. But 'hands in pockets' lad discovered a second wind and grabbed a broken bottle from the floor on his way out. Spotting this, I pushed him up against the wall and fired a brutal head butt into his face, hearing and feeling his jaw crack. I stepped back and fired a combination of shots that pushed him outside the doors and onto the floor, blood pissing out of everywhere. As he tried to get up I fired a steel-toe capped kick into his ribs, he wasn't going anywhere now. We closed the door and it was over, or at least that moment was over, but is it ever really over?

Rumours now started to do the rounds that these were Leicester lads and part of what was called the 'Baby Squad', a notorious group of football hooligans whose weapons of choice were small, plastic handled Stanley blades (craft knives) that they carried in a front jacket or shirt pocket. They had the reputation of walking around clubs slashing people's backs and walking on, leaving their victim puzzled as to why their back was stinging and their shirts soaked with blood. This was now the aftermath, the rumour mill kicking into gear. You have just dealt with the immediate threat only now to be contemplating the comebacks. Revenge has no statute of limitations and as with every altercation enemies are formed and often return. Sure enough, while walking around that night we found two Stanley blades on the floor where they had been mingling so we had good cause to believe they would return. Only next time they may be mob-handed.

The rest of that night passed relatively peacefully; it was now closing time and people were leaving in droves. I walked to my car that was parked just a few feet away from the Dog's back doors and reached for my kit bag that always sat on the front passenger seat. This bag contained everything I needed for training, including what I may need at the end of a shift on the door. As a karate instructor it wouldn't be out of the ordinary to have a bag in the car which contained a karate Gi, a belt and sparring gloves. It would also be reasonable to see pain spray, bandages, plasters and a mouth guard. Given that I also taught practical self-defence classes it wouldn't be much of a stretch to explain to anyone who may be inclined to ask, why my bag contained a pair of knuckle dusters, a baseball bat and a set of nun chucks. Did I use these weapons as props for class? Yes, I did and not because I needed to but because if I was ever questioned by the police about this collection of items in my car I would have plenty of people who could give evidence about their legitimacy. Reaching into my bag, that evening, I pulled out a pair of knuckle-dusters, slid them onto my hands and made my way back to the club where there was still a small crowd taking their time to drink up. There was no sign of anything about to kick off but the back doors were now open with groups of malingerers all over the place. If the lads from earlier were coming back tonight it would be around now. Kick-offs can and do happen at any time but closing time is known to spring the odd nasty surprise. I had put both my hands in my trouser pockets and the dusters were just at the end of my fingers should I need to slip them on.

As I walked through the club asking people to finish off their drinks and to make their way outside, my attention was drawn to a small group of lads who still had full pints left. They appeared to have no intention of knocking them back anytime soon. "Can you see your beers off, please lads, and make your way outside?" One of the lads lifted his glass to his mouth, sipped the tiniest bit of his beer, smiled at me then put his glass back down. "It's going to take you a long time to finish drinking like that." He picked up his glass and took another little sip, "I can take as long as I fucking want, I paid for it so no rush." This type of drinker is not uncommon, every bouncer has come face to face with the 'I will leave when I am ready' twat. Normally it's just the drink talking and they are not looking for any trouble so walking away and giving them time can be the best solution in most cases. I would have done exactly that if I hadn't heard him tell his mates that he was going to keep taking sips just to piss me off. I picked up his beer glass and put it on a table a few feet away and then told him that he needed to leave right now. "Go fuck yourself." BOOM! My forehead met his face with a ferocity that not only broke his nose but split his lip and cracked his orbital bone leaving him unconscious where he fell, his mates stood back and declared themselves as conscientious objectors and then promptly left the club leaving 'sippy-drink' guy lying there.

Wait, what, you hit someone just because he said, "Go fuck yourself"? It has been well documented that communication is 93% non-verbal, the words 'go fuck yourself' communicated only 7% of his intentions. Him leaning in and grinding his forehead on my cheek whilst reaching for his beer glass communicated the rest. Have you ever seen a glass pushed into someone's face? I eliminated the threat based on the information that he'd communicated to me. As a bouncer, as in life; split second decisions are made; decisions that you then spend the rest of your life questioning, because action and inaction both have consequences.

It was now 3am and I was home sitting by my three-year-old son's bed, watching him sleep. I'd always go in to kiss him good night when I got home from work having missed his bedtime and story time. He was fast asleep and looked so peaceful and beautiful, simply perfect. He was safe in his bed wrapped tightly in his Disney quilt, his arms clutching one of his favorite cuddly toys. 'Figment' was a stuffed animal, a character from Epcot in Orlando. 'If you can dream it, you can do it', was the well-known Epcot motto and as I'd watch my precious boy dreaming I too dreamt of a better, safer life for him. I'd often sit at his bedside, listen to his breathing and whilst doing so relive the night's earlier encounters. Tonight was no exception. I'd sat and contemplated what I would do to anyone who would hurt my child as I had done someone else's child that evening. Some might call it self-torture, to me it was cathartic. It kept me in touch with my humanity, it kept my feet firmly on the ground and the overwhelming empathy that I'd fought to hold back earlier in the night came flooding back with a vengeance as I sat sobbing like a baby. I then saw his eyes open and a big smile appear on his face, I'd dry my eyes once again. Daddy's home. He reached out for a hug and I squeezed him so tight. I swore on my life that I'd never let anyone hurt him.

"Total bollocks, bullshit! Nobody knocks out three men in a matter of seconds and who the fuck walks around with knuckle dusters in their pocket in anticipation of a kick off?" I can still recall at the age of 16, I had been involved in karate for about a year when I found myself in the company of a few older gentlemen who were friends with the lads I trained with. One of these old-timers was talking about his time in prison and how he had knocked out two prison guards. He'd served a hefty prison sentence for armed robbery, he just laughed and said, "I got a few more years for that." I just listened and thought, bollocks, this is just a 'Billy bullshit' making up stories!

It was incomprehensible to me that these older, family-men were not only career criminals but also hard as fucking nails. Sure I'd seen fighting at school and as you'll learn I'd had a few scuffles myself, but listening to these old fogies describe the kind of violent life that they had led just didn't compute. Every seasoned bouncer will listen to my encounters on the door, nod their head and say, "Yep, been there!" But just like my 16-year-old self, many people will find it hard to imagine that this type of world really exists and just like I had, will choose to see fiction; a true story embellished to make a good story. Welcome to *'Fighting with Myself'*, a story about finding strength and courage by creating alter-egos that took charge when the real me wanted to run and hide.

The very notion that one man could destroy three men with relative ease will have the average person quite baffled I'm sure. To most people this kind of ferocious violence is something that you would only see in a movie. You may have read this first chapter and be asking yourself if this story is in fact true, maybe it's just based on a true story but embellished to have the reader wanting to turn the page. Well, not only is this story accurate, it's also not as spectacular as it sounds, many bouncers reading this will be saying, "Welcome to my world."

By now you may be thinking that you have picked up a book that is just all about violence, 'please God no, not another tell-all bouncer book celebrating the life of yet another hard man who has taken revenge on all the people who have ever done him wrong over the years'. No, don't worry this isn't one of those. Yes, there are plenty of violent confrontations throughout these pages but that is because this book is about a battle with my violent alter ego, a personality that I created out of desperation. Scared of confrontations and fearful of the big bad world around me I desperately wanted to fit in, be somebody and just be able to walk in the neighbourhood without being worried about whom I may bump into. The man you just read about in this opening chapter isn't who I really am though, but rather somebody who I was able to become to complete a task. 'Necessity is the mother of invention' and my need to become confident and capable made me figure out a way, my way.

Chapter #2

Scared

I was born and raised in Willenhall, Coventry, a very working class, salt-of-the-earth community - a place that holds very fond memories for me. I lived on Meadfoot Road, situated less than a quarter of a mile from the Willenhall precinct. The Precinct was a place that many of us had to walk through to get to school but when I say 'walked' what I really mean is we 'ran the gauntlet'. The Precinct was ground-zero for bullies and thugs and was a place that scared the shit out of me. Our house, as children, was always filled with people whether it be mine or my brothers' friends, my parents' friends or just neighbours popping in to borrow some milk or sugar. Those were the days when you really could leave your doors open and the community looked out for each other. But kids were kids and the mutual respect that the adults had for each other wasn't always shared by younger heads who saw rivalry based on what school you attended or the sort of clothes you wore.

I attended Chace Primary School which was located at the bottom of Remembrance Road and only a short distance from Corpus Christi Primary School on Langbank Avenue. Corpus Christi was our school 'rivals' - well, the tough kids' rivals anyway. I would often hear about gangs from both schools meeting up for fights. I was far too scared to get involved in any of that but living in Willenhall meant you were always only one comment or gaze away from some kind of confrontation. By this point I'd accepted that I was always going to be a victim, doing whatever I could to stay under the bullies' radar. That tactic worked for the most part, give or take the odd, "Give me your sweets!" and the occasional pushing and shoving. In my mind this strategy was working; I just needed to let the bullies get away with it as I had no other choice, right?

Being scared, of course, is a human trait and something that everybody feels, but at such a young age I did believe it was only me that was experiencing this. I had absolutely no idea how to deal with or control that overwhelming feeling, so at the first sign of any trouble I would just leg it. "I am scared," was what I repeatedly told myself without any awareness that those thoughts were crippling me. I tried many times to not be scared but the feeling was so overpowering that it controlled me every time I was faced with any kind of confrontation.

I remember when I was about 8 years of age, I had gone to a small fete with some friends at a church located at the bottom of Remembrance Road and there was a stall there selling tries on blackout card. I don't remember how much it cost back then but I do remember handing over some pocket money that my Mum had given me. I picked a number. I was convinced I was going to win and desperately wanted to not miss the draw. I stood next to the table for about an hour or so until the winner was revealed. It came as no surprise to me that I had indeed picked the winning number and no sooner after the cash was handed over, me and a few friends were in the sweet shop on a spending spree.

Well, that was until a few troubled kids (as I called them) barged into the shop, stole our sweets and the rest of my winnings. One of my friends wasn't giving up his sweets quite so easily though and got a good kicking for his insubordination. The rest of us just legged it, leaving him to a beating. Even at such a young age, I do recall, a sea change was happening. The more violence and confrontations I experienced, the more I was starting to become a little desensitized to it and in later years I became very aware that the 'troubled' kids had a massive head start on me. I was only getting on this emotional rollercoaster (of violence) every now and then but they were on it every day, the biggest difference being that their dysfunctional family life put them in the driver's seat and they owned the ride; I was just a passenger.

Having your sweets and a bit of money taking off you by a group of young tearaways can quite easily be seen as just kids misbehaving, pushing their weight around, bullying etc. We can put whatever label we want on this behaviour but let's call this what it really is and stop trying to justify criminality by playing it down. I had just been mugged. I hadn't been hurt however as I had run away but my friend on the other hand got a good beating. Yes, we had been mugged. Running away had always worked for me and it had worked again, but of course it was only going to be a matter of time before the running option wasn't going to be available, and that time did come.

Rick, as we would call him, was a young lad who, along with other family members and associates, was always involved in some kind of trouble. His roguish behaviour wasn't that uncommon for a working-class, council estate upbringing. Even from an early age it was obvious that he was destined to be more than just a rogue and as was often the case, the prison system was his destiny.

Every young kid has those teenage indiscretions that are just part of growing up and eventually one grows out of. Stealing a bag of sweets from a shop or knocking on someone's window and legging it are, for most kids, as bad as it gets but this wasn't the case for Rick. I never really knew him personally, but very much knew who he was, and I'd seen him and his family around the estate. Everyone who lived in Willenhall knew of the family's reputation. Willenhall was full of rogues, scoundrels and bad boys, most of whom grew up and moved on but then there are always that small number who spent years in and out of young offenders' institutes, only to become fully fledged criminals by their early teens, most of whom then found it impossible to turn their lives around for the better.

I was about 12 years old. I remember standing at the bus stop on St James Lane. It was close to the White Bear pub and on the bend where St James Lane meets Remembrance Road. The bus stop had a shelter, a luxury in those days! It had a roof and Plexiglas windows, an important fact as it explains why the story I'm about to tell you went down the way it did. Rick approached the shelter from Remembrance Road. I saw him crossing the road and heading towards me. He was of a similar age to mine but a lot smaller and skinnier, yet he carried a confidence and attitude that made him very scary to me. I liken the feeling he gave me with how I later saw Joe Pesci in Casino. Ruthless and intimidating - he meant business! There's more to come about the real Joe Pesci in a later chapter.

Once at the shelter he started demanding money from me in a thick, Glaswegian accent. For those not familiar, Glaswegians can sound aggressive and scary, even when they are being friendly, so Rick didn't have to try too hard to have me shitting myself. He pushed me up against the Plexiglass, pulled out a knife from his pocket and put blade to my throat. "Gimme 10p!" he demanded. Agreed, it wasn't quite a major heist and if he wanted to make a career of mugging he was going to need to up his game a little, but yep that was what he demanded, 10p. There was zero chance of running away so I handed him everything I had in my pockets and he legged it. Whilst I can joke about it now, at the time, it was terrifying and for weeks had me questioning if there was really anything I could have done differently.

Was I now going to be known as the push-over, the kid who can be bullied? When would this shit happen to me again? Fortunately for me Rick's reign of terror was still in its infancy and nothing else came of our encounter, but as predicted he did 'up his game' in later years when he plunged a knife into the heart of one of his friends during a drunken argument, which as you'd imagine, resulted in a murder conviction and a hefty prison sentence. My fear of confrontations, for me at least were justified, I hadn't lived in an aggressive or violent household. Sure, I had fall-outs with my brothers but we never really got into fist fights, so real violence was very alien to me. The closest I'd really gotten to having a scrap at home was when I tried to stop my older brother tying me to the bed so he could fart on my face (dirty bastard, I'm still plotting my revenge!).

It wasn't until later years that I started to put it all together; the troubled kids didn't really have a chance. Violent fathers who to them, were seen as normal had steered these kids into a direction which people like me had no idea about, such as when I heard that my mate Andrew's dad had 'gone away'. I just assumed he'd gone on holiday. It wasn't until I got much older that I found out that Parkhurst wasn't exactly a holiday camp, so unlike many of these kids I wasn't subjected to beatings by a dad who came home pissed up every night or brothers who were in and out of jail. Most of these kids weren't really bullies or thugs, they had just been given a shit start in life and they, just like me, were trying to figure out their next move.

It was starting to become clear after the Rick encounter that just maybe I needed to change the fucking record. Telling myself I am scared, and I am weak had become a massive albatross around my neck, but it was going to take me another three years or so to shake this fucker off but shake it off I did.

Being scared is of course a human condition that we all have to deal with, but what does being scared even mean? Is being scared the same as being nervous, frightened or terrified? I could make things extremely easy for myself here as there are dozens of books on the subject of fear, so all I would really have to do is a little bit of plagiarisation and give you the textbook definition, but that isn't who I am or what I do. My experience has been real and my goal here is to share those experiences in my own words, in my own voice. I guess my earliest memory of what being scared felt like for me was at infant school, when I was asked to leave the classroom and go into the main hall where the big clock was located. Everybody in the class would be asked at some point to go to the clock, come back to the classroom and tell everybody what the time was. Not only is this a scary memory but also a happy one as I recall spending time sitting on my father's knee while he taught me what the hands on a clock meant.

"Ok, what's the time?" When I heard the teacher say this I got excited and hoped she would pick me. I recall sitting and sort of bouncing on my chair in an attempt to have the teacher look at me. "Ian, what's the time?"

Yes! I rushed excitedly out of the door, down the hall and found myself standing right in front of the big clock, "Ok, if the little hand is pointing to the one and the big hand is pointing to the one, the time is...." Oh no, I'd forgotten how it worked, surely the only thing it can be is; the time is one-one, right? No, that can't be right, Then I remembered something about it being, past or to the hour. Wait, I also remember it being o'clock at some point. That's it, I've got it. I rushed back into the class, stood at the front and proclaimed, "It's one, one o'clock Miss". The class started to clap and I felt like a superstar but then, "No Ian, that's not exactly right, can you go back out and try again, it's going to be either past the hour, or to the hour." Once again I rushed excitedly out the door to the clock thinking to myself, just add past or to and I would get it right, but when I looked at the clock the hands had moved. I went back into the classroom and told the teacher that the hands were not in the same place and I didn't know what the time was. Mrs E was a nice old lady. I say 'old', she was probably only in her twenties but to a 5-year-old she was old. She gave me a hug and a blue bird milk chocolate toffee and told me that I would get another try another day.

That evening I asked my dad to help me again, and this is when I started to realise what scared felt like, "The one is five, the two is ten, the three is 15; this is past the hour, this is to the hour." I wasn't getting it. My dad explained further, showing me that there were five digits between the twelve and the one, and ten digits between the twelve and the two but I recalled my mind just going blank and I couldn't see any numbers in my head at all. I started to panic so I just switched off and didn't want to try anymore.

The next day I went to school thinking I would panic again and go blank if I was asked to visit the clock, but this didn't happen. What did happen was even worse, another kid got the task and came back into the classroom within seconds and gave the correct answer, and then the next day another kid with the correct answer and the next day another kid with the correct answer. Was I now the only kid in the class who didn't understand this? It was at this point I started to realise that it was going to be easier to just hide from the things that

I was uncomfortable with and all the things that triggered what I later learned was an emotion called fear.

Was I actually scared though, or was this something else? Of course, I couldn't rationalize this feeling or understand what it meant. When this emotion arrived I did everything I could to make the feeling go away. When I anticipated being asked to do something that would make that feeling arrive, I would find a way to remove myself. An example of this would be asking to use the toilet if I thought I would have to read out loud, or do something naughty or disruptive so I would be sent out of the class thus achieving the same objective. Starting at very early age I had figured out how to divert attention away from myself or create some kind of chaos that made everybody look the other way and basically leave me alone. Scared, frightened or nervous, etc. were just words, words that meant absolutely nothing to me as a child. I only knew what these emotions felt like and what they did to me. I quickly learned how to make those emotions go away though, simply put, I started to live under the radar whenever possible. Making myself invisible was a skill I picked up pretty quickly. I of course didn't know what I was doing but I did know that what I was doing was working.

Let's use going to the clock as an example of something I wasn't comfortable with and something that triggered fear in me; when that emotion hit, I immediately worked on making the feeling go away. When I was asked to go to the clock I would go, wait a few seconds, return to the class and just make up what time it was. When I was told, "No that isn't correct," I would make a joke or do something silly to make the whole class laugh. Being the class clown for even just a few seconds removed the fear and replaced it with endorphins, the chemical associated with being happy and having fun. Of course, I had no idea at that time what was happening, I just knew that it worked.

It didn't take long before the teacher just gave up asking me to do anything, as to do so resulted in a class disruption. Yes, as early as at five years of age I had awakened an alter ego who I'd used to take care of me; he'd done a great job looking after me as a child, but as I matured so did he and consequently, so did the way in which he wanted to handle situations.

Chapter #3

The Liar

I cast my mind back to Binley Park Comprehensive school when I was around the age of fourteen. Like most tutor groups, mine was made up of students with mixed academic abilities, brought together first thing every morning before we branched off into our appointed academic ability classes. I was in one of the low academic performance groups based on my test results from primary school. I never found school easy and was a pretty slow learner. In fact, school scared me! It wasn't a place I ever really felt comfortable nor a place I felt I belonged; even to this day entering a school triggers a level of anxiety for me.

Occasionally, during tutor group time, the teacher would play a game where students in the group were assigned a specific number. The teacher would then give the group a task to perform; for example, draw a picture of a house and then call out two numbers. If your number was called, you needed to race to the front of the class and complete the task on the blackboard. I was really good at art, I felt at ease with it and loved drawing so this type of task was right up my street. Unfortunately, one of the tasks also involved spelling, something I was not only crap at but massively embarrassed by my inability to navigate the written word. When a spelling task was called followed by my number I'd pretend not to hear so I could get away with not doing it. This worked for a while until one day the teacher realised what I was doing, stopped the game and called me out by name to spell a word of his choosing. To this day I can still remember the feeling of overwhelming dread and just wanting to be physically sick. The idea of standing in front of the class in my most vulnerable state was crushing. Needless to say, the whole incident resulted in the class and the teacher laughing at me and a horrendous feeling that the walls were closing in as a stifling panic attack set in. Yet again, fear taking a hold, I needed to get the fuck out of that room. I got up and ran out of the class, the laughter of the other children echoing through the walls of the corridors.

I fled across the school grounds feeling embarrassed and stupid. I'd decided to head home but just before I got to the school gate I was spotted by a teacher who we'll call Mr. H. Mr. H was a bit of a hippy, an art teacher who also taught filmmaking. Art was my favourite subject and I loved his class. When I'd reached the back of one of the buildings on my way to the gate Mr. H was sitting on the floor having a cheeky cigarette, he asked if I was ok. I confided in him about what had happened and how the teacher had humiliated me in front of everyone on purpose. Mr. H was different from all the other teachers. He had an ease about him which immediately made me feel comfortable enough to talk honestly to him. In that moment he felt like someone who was more of a friend than a teacher and someone who would do their best to help me. Once I had told him what had happened he revealed that he was, 'shit at spelling too, in fact, shit at most things'. He then gave me what is probably the best advice I have I have ever been given. 'Understand these three rules, they will make your life so much easier'. One - make humility your best friend. Two - don't hide your weaknesses, admit them and face them, and, Three, never, ever lie to yourself.

After chatting with Mr. H I jumped on the bus and headed home, the incident in the classroom playing over and over in my head. I knew I was going to be walking into that same tutor group in the morning and I knew I would have to face everyone who had laughed at me. I wasn't looking forward to it. However, Mr. H had really got me thinking, 'Don't hide your weaknesses, admit them and face them.' I really wasn't sure I could do either, so I spent most of that night wide awake, putting together a bullshit story that I could use in the next day's tutor group. I needed to think of something that would explain why I had stormed out of the class.

I had decided I was going to get into class early and have a chat with the tutor group teacher before any other students arrived. When I got there however, there were already a good few in the class. I was shitting myself. I had spent the past twenty-four hours essentially creating an elaborate lie that would make me look like the hero and the teacher look like a bully, but then, in that moment, I decided that I would just take the hit and deal with the consequences whatever they may be. I had been hiding my weaknesses and had been lying to myself for many years but Mr. H was right, this shit had to stop. I had planned on telling everyone that I'd had a heavy cold and that my ears had been blocked so I didn't hear what the teacher was saying, but the more I went over this story in my head the more I heard myself sounding like a total loser. Why did I have to make up a story? Why isn't the truth good enough? These questions were about to be answered as I had decided to just be honest.

On entering the classroom, I fully expected to be ridiculed and made fun of, but nothing was said. I went to my seat and as more kids came in I waited for someone to say something, but nothing. I'd had a sleepless night worrying about this day but no-one seemed to remember what had happened. I continued to sit there, waiting for something. I decided that I wasn't going to wait any longer, so I went up to the front of the class and asked the teacher if I could have a word about what had happened yesterday. I said that I needed to apologise for storming out of the class but first I wanted to tell him why. "I am not a very confident speller," I said, "you put me on the spot and I was embarrassed, I just needed to get out of the classroom." The teacher was surprisingly gracious in his reply, he said that Mr. H had already spoken to him and that it was he who needed to apologise to me. It had been a lesson for him about recognising each student's ability. He then said, "It must have taken a lot for you to come and speak to me, well done for finding the courage."

It really hadn't registered with me at that time what I'd just done. Not only did I show up in a class where I was expecting to face a lynch mob but I showed up with only the truth as my weapon to fight them off with. It was around maybe a week or so later when someone did ask about what had happened in the tutor group and why I'd stormed out. I found myself almost by default starting to lie but I quickly corrected myself. I responded by saying, "I am not comfortable standing up and writing and I am not very good at spelling. When I was called up I felt embarrassed so I left the room." As the truth left my lips, I had an overwhelming feeling of calm and for the first time in my young life I felt crazy confident and in control. It was as though I had just been given a super power but at only fourteen years of age I had no idea what I was experiencing - until the day I was late for school and hadn't completed my homework. When challenged about both, instead of lying my way out of it, I was honest and said, "Well I stopped off at the sweetshop! That's why I was late, and I never completed my homework because I played out on my bike instead." The teacher said, "Well at least you are honest," and then promptly gave me a three-day, after school detention.

Fast forward a few years and I was watching an episode of a TV programme called Tales of the Unexpected. A verger, who ran a small local parish, was called in to see the parish elders and informed that he would have to begin communicating with the parish via letters and telephone, learning a new system of communication. Feeling embarrassed, he had to reveal to the elders that he could not read or write and could not do as they wished. The elders made life difficult for him and he was forced to resign. Now, his wife was a very good baker and the verger himself was a stickler for professional service, so combining their skills, they decided to open their own top-class tearooms. One day, an American businessman visited them and was so impressed that he wanted to license the tearoom brand and open them up all over the US. They agreed to the deal and the former verger was given documents to sign. He tells the businessman that he is illiterate, to which he smiles and says, "So you're telling me you have built this amazing business without being able to read or write?" "That's correct," he replies. "Well imagine what you could be if you had learned to read and write," the American responded. The verger replies, "I know exactly what I would be, I would still be a verger." And there it was, right there. Make humility your best friend, don't hide your weaknesses, admit them and face them, and never, ever lie to yourself. Thank you, Mr. H, you have no idea how you shaped my life.

Chapter #4

It's all just an act

"That's what I like about this agency," says Trigger, "they insist on complete honesty." Boycie asks, "So you told them you are a road sweeper?" "No," replies Trigger, "I told them I was a bus inspector." "Why?" asks Rodney. Trigger adds, rubbing his hands together, "To add a bit of glamour!" Del Boy, of course, jumps in on the act when he signs up to the same dating agency, calling himself 'Derek Duval', the Managing Director of an import/export company and claims to drive a Ferrari. Even Raquel embellished the truth with her dating profile which described her as an actress, yet she was a part-time strip-o-gram. The genius that drew so many of us to the inimitable Only Fools and Horses, was that the characters were all so believable, they represented us. Just like all of us, they strived to be better versions of themselves and to coin a lyric from a musical classic, 'All we have to do now, is take these lies and make them true, somehow'.

By now, you may have guessed that I am a huge fan of Only Fools and Horses. I remember being blown away the first time I saw the cast being interviewed out of character; it felt strange to separate the cast from their roles. David Jason who played Del Boy, the leading role, was so far removed from the wheeling and dealing, lovable rogue portrayed on screen which highlighted his incredible acting talent. Buster Merryfield who played Uncle Albert was a bank manager for most of his adult life and in his youth was a very talented boxer, yet in the show he's Del and Rodney's white-bearded, old uncle hailing from Tobacco Road, East London. In the industry, it's called acting. In fact what is really happening is that they're adopting roles for a short period of time whilst the cameras are rolling and then back to their familiar lives and roles when the cameras turn off.

Recruiting the help of a different side to one's personality (an alter ego) is nothing unusual. In fact it's absolutely necessary in everyday life. The absence of this ability would, to some extent, leave anyone baffled as to what to do in certain situations. Everyday tasks could become very difficult. Parents have to become disciplinarians, often dishing out tough love when every part of their soul just wants to show compassion. Police and firefighters must go into professional 'mode' when dealing with an emergency call and can't let their natural emotions get in the way. Athletes work hard on their psychological development as much as their physical, in order to allow them to get 'in the zone' and even the average Joe knows how to put their 'work-head' on. By now I'd become an actor, not in the professional sense of course but an actor nonetheless. You are also an actor, we're all actors. William Shakespeare once said, "All the world's a stage and all the men and women merely players. They have their exits and their entrances; and one man in his time plays many parts." For me, however, it had become far more than just acting. I was now deliberately and consciously creating separate personalities to deal with different situations. Yes, I acted brave when I was scared and happy when I was sad, but everybody does this... right? What I'm talking about is something else though.

1973 and a very normal, typical day in that equally normal, typical comprehensive school in Coventry; what was going to happen to me however was anything but normal. Jay was your typical school bully who took pleasure in making other kid's lives miserable; usually with the typical name calling, pushing, shoving and general taunting. One morning, for no apparent reason to me, Jay sauntered over and said, "Me and you in the toilets, dinner time, square go!" My heart sank and I flushed red hot. I can still recall all these years later, my body going into complete shock as dread devoured me; fight or flight took a grip, as tunnel vision made everything else around me appear blurred. Yes, I was scared and as always I tried so desperately not to be but this time was different, instead of fighting with the emotion I just accepted it and let it wash over me, letting it do its thing. I knew instantly that this wasn't one of those situations that I was going to be able to blag my way out of and I spent the next few hours, which felt like weeks, searching for a solution. Eventually, with only half an hour to go, I resigned myself to the fact that this would in fact be happening and I was surprised to feel a sense of acceptance. 'Fuck it, how bad can it really be?' Honestly, what was the worst that could happen? Just steam in and don't stop. It was as though the torment had flicked a switch and nobody, including me, knew what might happen next. The adrenaline that Jay's challenge had released had awakened something, someone in me that I never knew existed, or did I? Was this now my alter ego making an appearance again?

The bell rang at lunchtime, and I remember being terrified but also strangely excited, what would the next ten minutes bring? As another sudden rush of adrenaline took hold, I strode down to the front of the class where Jay was sitting and calmly said, "See you in the loo." I arrived there first with Jay not too far behind. He had told his friends to stay outside which made me feel worse. It was now just the two of us with no one watching. No words were exchanged and before I had a chance to gather my thoughts Jay landed the first shot. He was all over me, his arms flailing around like a fucking windmill. I didn't even try to fight back, I didn't even really know how to throw a punch and as it turned out neither did this moron. Instinctively, I covered my head while this human windmill wore himself out and in the blink of an eye, it was all over. I just remember wondering what the fuck was that was all about? Was that really it? All this time I had been scared of what a fight felt like and that was it? I still remember the mixture of emotions, it was like shitting yourself while standing in the queue for a theme park ride only to be desperate to get straight back on once the ride was over. I understood even more now how the troubled kids had dealt with confrontations because they were doing this shit all the time and the adrenaline that crippled me actually excited them to some degree.

I had always seen Jay as the tough kid in school although that illusion had now been shattered, I now looked at him differently. He certainly still looked and carried himself like that bully but now I also saw a sad, pathetic pretender, so much so that I approached him later that day and said, "I want another shot, same time tomorrow?" "Yeah let's do it," was his response. The next day arrived but Jay didn't. In fact, he wasn't in school for the rest of that week. I'd had the illusion that Jay was a fighter, a good one at that given that no one at school wanted to fuck with him. Upon reflection I'd never actually seen him fighting with anyone though, I'd only ever seen him picking on people who always backed down. I had called his bluff when I had met him in the school toilets, it hadn't gone down the way he expected and he wasn't happy. Although he wasn't at school the rest of that week, word got back to me that this wasn't over and that I should be expecting him to be in my face outside of school someday, but I had other ideas. I wasn't about to be controlled by this fat twat and spend time worrying about when and where he would show up, so I decided to take control of what happened next. I wanted to find out where he lived and pay him a visit.

It was a Saturday morning, me and a few friends were out on our bikes when a friend of Jay's came over on his bike, "So you want to know where Jay lives then?" Fuck me, the grapevine has been busy! "Yeah, I hear he has been telling people that he is going to beat me up." The lad gave me his address, "So when should I tell him to expect you?" My heart sank and that crazy sick feeling hit me like a speeding train. I heard myself starting to mumble with an obvious nervousness and a quivering in my voice. There it was again, I didn't want this lad to see how scared I was so I kept dialogue sparse, I took a deep breath and tried to compose myself. Fuck it, let's do it right now! I wanted this awful feeling to go away and the only way to do that was either bottle it and go back to running away from shit, or confront it and get it over with.

The address that this lad had given me wasn't that far away, probably less than half a mile. We didn't have mobile phones back then so this lad wasn't able to make a call and let Jay know we were heading his way and I wasn't about to let this lad get there before us to give Jay the heads up. Just to be clear I wasn't heading over there feeling like an experienced fighter. I hadn't suddenly gained some kind of crazy fighting ability. I had, however, obtained a strange confidence and to some degree, an ignorance about what having a fight was really all about, even though I'd been training at the Coventry boys' club in both boxing and a martial art called Aikido. When I say training, what I really mean is playing, it wasn't a serious attempt at becoming a good fighter; it was just a place where I met my friends and it was more about the fun element than it was about learning a skill.

When I thought about it, it was the boxing training I'd done that I credited for the result in my last encounter with Jay. I'd learnt how to cover up and evade punches and although I hadn't done much in the way of sparring, I'd learnt how not to get hit, at least. To say that I was shitting myself is an understatement. I was terrified and had no idea what I was going to do. I had no idea about what the outcome would be but I did know that I had to confront this lad and I had to learn to control this shitty feeling that arrived every fucking time. I felt just like every kid who has ever been bullied. I was you, the person who had lost sleep worrying about dealing with what problems tomorrow would bring, but I also knew that this was a problem that I had to confront and if I was to bottle this it would only make things worse down the road. I would become a prisoner of my own weakness; a prisoner of my own fears. I wasn't going to let that happen anymore. We all got on our bikes and headed to the address. Nobody spoke a word the entire way, I certainly wasn't able to speak even if I'd wanted to. My mouth and throat had become bone-dry as the rush of adrenaline took hold and threatened to beat me before I had even stepped into the ring, metaphorically speaking.

As I approached Jay's house my heart raced faster and faster, I had literally no idea about what I was going to do but I thought I had the advantage this time given that it was me calling the shots now. There was no real winner last time, although I kind of felt like a winner. I'd survived pretty much unscathed but of course I expected this time was going to be different. When we arrived we saw Jay's mate, the lad who had given me the address, was already there, sitting on a wall like someone who'd bought a front-row ticket to his favourite show. We didn't know if he had already told Jay that we were on our way and we started to think we had been set up to be 'jumped', but we needn't have worried as it turned out this lad wasn't even Jay's friend, he'd just heard about our situation and wanted to watch a fight.

I walked up the pavement that led to Jay's front door. I stood and hesitated for a while as every part of me wanted to just turn around and walk away. Knock, knock, knock. I waited but nobody came to the door. After some time I turned and started to walk away whilst telling myself that I had shown up, I was there and could hold my head up and say - I was there. But that wasn't good enough for me, this wasn't going to be over until I had confronted him. Fuck it! Knock, knock, knock. A few more seconds passed then through the frosted glass in the front door window pane I saw movement and the door opened. It was Jay, he just looked at me, clearly taken by surprise that I was on his doorstep. I had to do a double-take, was it him or was it somebody else? I'd only seen him in a school uniform. It wasn't that he looked different, he just looked bigger, well, fatter than I remembered. As we both stood there, I had a flashback of the last time we both faced off, that time he had launched at me without warning and I wasn't falling for that again. BOOM…. My fist hit his face square-on but did absolutely fuck all. Well, that's not completely true, I did inflict some damage to one of my own fingers, it swelled up like a balloon! Then I found myself on the floor with this huge, heavy fucker sitting on me and punching me in the face. I desperately tried to escape, he was far too heavy and far too strong, but then I managed to break free just enough to sink my teeth into his arm. He screamed out in pain so I bit down even harder and, unsurprisingly, he jumped off me.

Now we were both standing up and given I'd turned up at his doorstep it was time for me to put on a bit of show. The little boxing training I'd done allowed me to at least pretend that I knew what the fuck I was doing. Visualising how a boxer moves, I began, sort of, shadow boxing, acting like I was super-confident. Thankfully this was enough to make Jay back off. I was right, he was just a bully. He used his size and scary demeanor to make people believe he was something he wasn't. But now, hopefully, he thought that he was in a proper fight. I'd confronted my fears and I'd confronted the biggest bully in the school, but it wasn't my ability to have a fight that I was happy with, I still had no clue about that. It was my ability to act that I was most impressed with. I had become someone else for just a short period and the person I'd become was somehow believable!

I started to think that maybe I could become this person again and again, whenever I needed to be. Now that I'd discovered that acting a particular way in these types of situations was enough to have people believe what you were showing them, I wanted this to be real. I didn't feel comfortable that it was just an act, just an illusion - smoke and mirrors that I used to disguise the real me. But isn't this what everyone does? TV and movie actors spend their entire life pretending to be someone else. This wasn't a movie though; this was real life. Pretending and acting was only going to get me so far.

This was the early seventies, an era that saw the rise of the skinheads and the suede heads, the latter basically being a classier dressed thug. Red Doc Martin boots, a black Harrington jacket that had the tartan inlay, a Crombie overcoat and turned-up jeans that sat just at the top of my boots had now become my fashion statement. They were usually accompanied by a Ben Sherman shirt, complete with a pleat running down the back, topped off with a feather cut hairstyle. I found myself belonging to a subculture of which I had no understanding but in those days you were either a skinhead, a suede head or a nobody; or at least that's what I thought.

Having now taken on the school bully twice I'd become a minor celebrity, in my own head at least. I was being carried on the shoulders of the village peasants, having slayed the ogre, so-to-speak, and in the blink of an eye I'd become somebody. Just wearing those clothes not only separated me from the nobodies but made me feel accepted by everybody else who dressed the same. In my mind I'd now joined an elite group of people by doing nothing more than changing my appearance but I felt alive. I was excited about each new day ahead and I felt confident in my new skin. Of course it was still just an act, I may have looked the part but I was still fighting with who I really was and where I belonged. I'd put those three rules that Mr. H had told me about on the back burner for now as they were getting in the way. The confidence I was experiencing was far too powerful to let go of, the people in front of me were believing what I was showing them. I was Ace Face from the movie Quadrophenia. The movie didn't come out until many years later, but when I watched it I could totally relate. Ace Face was a character played by Sting, a hotel bellboy whose alter ego was a super-cool mod who rode a silver Vespa, living a lie that made him the most popular guy in the crowd. I'd had the fight with Jay and although it didn't go very well I'd embraced the experience and viewed it as a stepping stone to becoming someone. I'd now done away with that kid who ran from everything, the child who had used comedy to distract people's attention was now doing the complete opposite.

My confident demeanour was gaining attention but not always in a positive way. I had made the mistake of thinking that looking and behaving confident was enough to scare off the bullies but I was only just a little bit right.

Most bullies were only pretenders themselves, sitting in the ivory towers that they'd built out of fear and intimidation, feeling protected because most people ran from them. These same bullies were now leaving me alone. I wasn't presenting myself as an easy target now so they gave me a wide berth. Yeah, I felt like someone and I loved it, but just like Ace Face in the movie, it was still just an act and it was only a matter of time before I got busted.

Chapter #5

I am Someone

I can recall sitting on a warm, concrete paving slab at the front of our house on a hot sunny day, around the age of seven years. I was engrossed in watching my older brother fixing his bike when suddenly I felt a tiny ant exploring my leg, I hurriedly flicked it off. My brother noticed and asked, 'Do you want to see something really cool?' He sat down next to me and pulled a magnifying glass from his pocket. Positioning it so that the sun would create a home-made laser beam onto the paving slab, he pointed it at the poor, unsuspecting ant who was now scurrying around in the glare of the beam and starting to burn. He handed me the magnifying glass and filled with intrigue, I pointed it at the back of my hand to see if I could recreate the same effect on myself. Feeling my mistake instantly I soon decided against it. Realising the discovery of this new and amazing trick, I began to look for other things to burn, and as cheeky younger brothers do, I pointed it at the tyre on my brother's bike while he wasn't paying attention and was rather pleased with myself as I watched it start to smoulder. It was taking far too long to burn a hole though so I moved off to find other unsuspecting victims.

My mum came out to see what we were up to and I told her about my exciting discovery. In no uncertain terms, she told me it was cruel and if the other ants found out what I was up to they'd all gang up on me while I was asleep and take their revenge. At the age of seven, there was no reason why I wouldn't wholeheartedly believe everything my mum told me, including the reason I must never play by the local river.

She'd told me and my three brothers that 'The Vords' lived down there. Vords were monsters who disguised themselves as pancakes and sat on the side of the river and when kids went to pick them up they would turn back into monsters and eat the kids! Whenever there was a news item in the local paper or on TV about a child going missing my mum would say, "See, I told you, eaten by the Vords!" We had an ant infestation in the house one summer and I remember her saying, "They've come looking for you!" In hindsight, I know she was trying to keep us safe, keep us on the straight and narrow, but her imagination was pure genius.

My brother had a friend whose special talent was being able to burp extremely loudly, in fact his nickname was Micky burp. He'd fallen off his bike and broken his arm, yet my mum told me it had broken because he burped too loudly. Apparently, whilst he'd been watching the TV he let out a huge burp which resulted in his arm snapping off and falling to the floor! It took the doctors a week to sew it back on. Most people will recall being told that if you pull a funny face when the wind changes, you'll stick like it, so it seemed perfectly logical to me that the ant that my brother had lasered was indeed plotting his revenge.

As a young child, I had already subconsciously begun to worry about the big, bad world out there. Holy crap, pancakes that turned into Vords and ants that were going to gang up on me - is it any wonder that I perceived the world as a very scary place that I needed to be able to run away from? My perception however, was and always would be my reality, but more often than not my perception in my youth at least, was totally wrong. As a teenager I didn't understand the difference between facts and opinions and like most people just accepted that my opinion was indeed a fact. Let me explain, it was a fact that Jay was big and powerful and that he was a bully, but it was only my opinion that he was actually capable and unbeatable.

Everything started to change when I realised that opinions can be subjective but facts are facts. For the longest time I'd had confidence confused with ability and believed that anyone who looked the part could do the 'biz', so to speak. I had confronted and had a fight with one of the school's biggest bullies and I was really starting to understand what confidence really meant and it wasn't what most people believed it to be.

'Gobshite' as we'll call him, was walking up and down the bus looking for victims. He would stop abruptly in front of one kid's seat, "Open your mouth, open your fucking mouth!" The kid, his latest victim, would be forced to sit back with his mouth open while Gobshite would take a deep breath, snorting snot from his nose into his throat and spit it into the poor kid's open mouth sitting in front of him. Gobshite was a well-known bully at Binley comprehensive and all the kids on the bus were shit scared of him. I'd previously adopted the opinion that kids like Gobshite, just like Jay, couldn't be beaten and I'd put them on a pedestal.

Gobshite's confidence and swagger put him in a different category to all the other kids on the bus. Well, at least that's what I thought as he sauntered past me looking for his next victim and then suddenly stopped, turned round and walked back towards me. My heart sank. It was obvious that I was next. I sat there shitting myself, contemplating having to swallow his snot in my own mouth and feeling physically sick with fear. But having already dealt with Jay, I had decided that this wasn't going to happen. All of a sudden this other kid approached us from the front of the bus. Seeing him approach, Gobshite stepped away from me and sat himself down in the nearest empty seat. This kid looked scrawny, small in stature and at least a year or two below him at school, but Gobshite appeared to know him, his presence seemed to subdue him. BANG! An almighty punch smashed into Gobshite's face followed by more punches that left him unconscious on the grubby floor of the bus. I couldn't believe my eyes, this kid had floored the bully and calmly walked back to his seat. Gobshite, the bully that everyone on the bus had feared had just been destroyed by a skinny little 'nobody'. He never even put up a fight, what the fuck did I just watch? It turned out that this kid wasn't a nobody, he was an exceptionally good schoolboy boxer and was part of a notorious local family. I later learned that he'd been expelled from his previous school in Liverpool and had moved with his family down to Coventry as his dad was now working at the 'Roots' car factory in Ryton.

Gobshite was lying face down on the floor and he wasn't moving. The skinny kid from Liverpool walked back to where he lay, bending over him he calmly said, "I fucking hate bullies, tell your brother he's next!" The rest of us stared at each other, open-mouthed at what we had just witnessed. I later found out that Gobshite's brother had been taking the piss out of this lad's younger sister for being the new 'fat' kid in school, so he had an axe to grind and he definitely meant business. Seeing the way Gobshite had been destroyed had awakened in me an even greater desire to understand my own potential. I imagined myself as that kid from Liverpool, I loved the notion of being able to do the 'do' without a song and dance. This lad's calm demeanour, whilst doing the business, was intriguing to me and it was this very incident that kicked off my quest for enlightenment. Becoming the person that could deliver this type of violence wasn't going to be easy though. In fact, seeing the ferociousness of this attack as a child had sickened me and just like every other kid on that bus I was terrified by it. But now after seeing this I found myself lying in bed at night, eyes closed, picturing myself on a huge movie screen. I would visualise myself as one of the tough kids and imagine how it felt to have people respecting me. I had now made this visualisation ritual a nightly thing, each night I'd close my eyes, let my mind go blank and then watch myself deal with every confrontation that I'd run away from. Of course, at the time I had no idea that my visualisation ritual was far more than just a kid trying to navigate his way around self-doubt and insecurities. I'd started to discover that I could achieve whatever I believed through visualisation. This nightly ritual was awakening what I had just called alter egos, personalities who would then sit quietly in the background waiting to be summoned.

I had now begun to glorify violence with the help of TV and movie superheroes who always won and looked so cool while doing it, but now having seen how inglorious real violence is up close I didn't want anything to do with it, or did I? I had an ongoing mental battle inside my head. I'd say to myself, 'Yes, I want to know how to do this,' but on the other hand be saying, 'No, don't get involved', my mind flipping between 'Yes, you can be strong and confident' to 'No, some people are just not made that way and that's OK'.

There is an old Native American parable about two wolves fighting inside a man's soul. One wolf was evil, full of anger, envy, greed, self-pity, and resentment. The other was full of love, kindness, empathy, generosity, truth and compassion. The story was being told by a grandfather to his grandchild. "So, who wins the battle?" the grandchild asked. "The one you feed," he replies. On a personal level, this served as a powerful reminder of the fight that every human being must face, regardless of what type of person you believe yourself to be or what type of life you lead. You will always find yourself battling conflicting emotions at some point in your life. This parable, it's very interesting to me, because it addresses the idea that we keep emotions alive by giving them attention (feeding them). I'd now, even at the age of only fourteen, started to take a very close look at when an emotion arrived, what prompted it and how long it stayed. When I got angry for example, I made a mental note of what made anger arrive, how long that anger lasted and what made it go away. I did exactly the same with literally every emotion and concluded that emotions were really just alter egos, separate personalities that could be fed or starved. This was how I was now framing emotions, and it made perfect sense to me, if emotions arrive, stay for a while then leave, I will just view them as alternate personalities, separate alter egos that needed to be controlled.

While walking around school the following day I saw a thousand plus kids, all potential victims to a handful of bullies like Gobshite and Jay. Well fuck that, not me! Yes, I will feed the good wolf as I enjoy being kind, caring and compassionate but the wolf inside me who was capable of being ruthless and dangerous was now going to be fed just enough to stay alive because I was now going to be 'someone'. I questioned though, what does that even mean? To me all it really meant was I wasn't going to continue being a nobody and now that I had confronted Jay and had also seen Gobshite destroyed, my perception of the world was starting to change and so was I, I was done with running and hiding and was now ready to stand up for myself. I had a bunch of emotions (alter egos) all fighting inside me, but it was me who was in control and not them. The first ego that really needed training though was the one who would teach me how to fight.

Chapter #6

The Fighter

By the age of eighteen I'd become a good, all-round, competitive karate fighter, and I'd acquired or so I had thought, the ability to have a scrap on the street should the situation present itself. I was sparring at the club most days and was dominating most of the club sessions. I'd taken up karate aged fifteen after watching a Bruce Lee movie. I was absolutely fascinated with the whole martial arts scene.

It was a Friday evening and we had just finished a tough workout. One of the lads suggested that we head into town for a night out, however we didn't have 'going out' clothes with us, just jeans, t-shirt and trainers. Back in the late 1970's and 80's you had no chance of getting into a nightclub without following the required dress code which was trousers, dress shirt and shoes. Luckily one of the lads knew a bouncer at a place called the Top Spot in Coventry and he said we were sure to get in. I still remember vividly how we all shared the karate club's small bathroom, stripping off and passing round the only bar of soap and negotiating the only working tap to wash ourselves with freezing cold water. We hopped on the bus from Holbrooks to Pool Meadow bus station in the city centre and started to make our way towards the nightclub. To this day I can't remember how we managed to get split up but five of us became two by the time we reached Corporation Street.

Heading across town, Tony and I had stopped and waited outside the Smithfield pub for the other three to join us. Tony was an old school friend who'd recently started training with us, a total beginner who, he himself would say, had two left feet and the coordination of Mr. Bean. As we looked around for our friends we could hear the muffled sound of music coming from the pub, along with chatting punters. They were just the normal sounds of the usual bustling, city nightlife yet just hearing this caused me some anxiety at the time. I'd always managed to put on the face of someone who was comfortable in these situations but the reality was I was still working on my confidence and although I forced myself to go into pubs and clubs, I always felt a little anxious. This anxiety was something that I'd really started to work on and I was getting better with. I'd like to think nobody would have guessed that I'd been battling with my confidence though, as I had over the years become very good at putting on an act.

It was about a year prior to this Top Spot night that I'd been away in Bournemouth with a few lads I worked with. We were ready for a night of clubbing and I recall thinking how my clothes looked ridiculous compared to the smart mature older lads I was with. I still hadn't outgrown the suede head look. I'd have been seventeen at the time while most of the other lads were in their early twenties. They all looked cool in their designer shirts and trousers while I looked like a complete fool in a t-shirt and baggy trousers that had foot-long docker pockets on each side and a four-inch waistband! Needless to say I had to borrow clothes from the other lads before they agreed to be seen in a pub with me. I recall being crazy-envious of them as they walked confidently into clubs and had a great time while I had to put on a brave face to pretend I was just like them. Although I did feel a little more comfortable in my new attire, the clothes 'maketh the man' as they say. I bring up Bournemouth because I am sure this is when I really broke out of my shell. I'd never been on an all-dayer followed by another all-dayer followed by five more of the same, but it really did the trick. I returned to Coventry with a totally new mindset and of course an application form for a Topman store card!

Now here I was a year later waiting for the rest of the lads outside of the Smithfield pub with Tony. After 5 mins we still couldn't see them so we continued walking along Corporation Street until we were stopped in our tracks by a complete stranger, fast approaching us head-on with a menacing and aggressive look on his face. He meant business as he walked towards me, stopping just inches from my face. He had a look, a look which told me if I opened my mouth whatever I said would be wrong and he'd take his shot. I knew if I tried to walk away he'd follow me. I was trapped. In that moment a tunnel vision emerged, everything else became a blur and in a split second I found myself in that situation which only ever happened to other people. Flashing thoughts raced through my mind, who was this guy, what did he want, what was he going to do? With each passing second I could feel my legs getting heavier like lead weights that simply refused to move as I attempted to reposition myself a step away from him. A feeling of nausea engulfed me, just like it had when I'd been asked to run up to the blackboard and spell a random word, only a lot worse this time. Fear and panic swept through me which seemed to last forever but was probably only a few seconds. I remembered what was triggering this intense response.

At the age of fifteen I'd spent two weeks in hospital having had a cartilage removed in my right knee. I had been put on Philip Ward at Coventry & Warwickshire Hospital which was the city's A&E (Accident and Emergency) ward at that time. I'd had the operation during the afternoon but that evening saw me still very drowsy. In and out of sleep throughout a night that seemed never-ending, I was awoken by the arrival of a new patient who was placed in the bed opposite me. He cried and moaned throughout the night and repeatedly called for the nurse. I still remember how slowly this night dragged on, with the sound of faint voices in the distance, the occasional snoring patient and the smell of food cooking which in hindsight was most probably just me hallucinating.

When the morning did eventually arrive I was able to see this lad sitting up in his bed directly opposite me. He was in a proper state, his face was battered and bruised and he had a very long visible line of stitches from his left ear running diagonally down his neck to his chest. I sat back and listened to his conversations with the bloke in the next bed. He described how he had been walking alone from the Locarno nightclub that previous night when out of the blue he was jumped by two men and had his throat cut. He'd lost several pints of blood and the doctors had been concerned he would bleed out and not make it. That encounter in the hospital had stayed with me and was engraved in my mind; seeing his parents sat sobbing at his bedside, his mother hysterical and his father in a seething rage, both kissing and hugging their boy as they prayed for his recovery. I'd heard the police take a statement whilst I pretended to be asleep. It turned out he was just nineteen years of age and if the ambulance crew hadn't been on the ball he would have died right there on the cold and wet fucking pavement. With no way out, bang!!

The bloke in front of me was head butted at least four times. As the fear and adrenaline started to take over and render me helpless, I used it to be devastatingly ruthless and take control of how the coming seconds would play out. I'd grabbed him by the shirt and wood-pecked the face off him. He dropped to the floor, nose busted across his face, blood covering the pavement, he wasn't unconscious but he wasn't getting up straight away either. He got on all fours and tried to crawl away then attempted to stand up, he could do neither, so I kicked him in the face and he rolled over onto his back. My friend, Tony, stood there shitting himself, he couldn't speak and overwhelmed with adrenaline, I wasn't much better, so I just legged it and Tony followed. As we ran I vividly remember what I can only describe as an out-of-body experience. I didn't destroy that guy, someone else did that. Now as I ran, a voice in my head was telling me, 'now Ian, that's how you deal with shit'. It was so surreal, something I couldn't begin to explain. Eventually my legs couldn't carry me anymore and after gathering ourselves again we made our way to the Top Spot, where sure enough our mates were waiting outside for us.

My t-shirt was covered in blood and I was seriously shaken up. I had no intention of going into the club now, I just wanted to go home. I felt overwhelmed and just wanted to get the fuck out of town. As we chatted, I looked over towards the doors of Top Spot just as an argument was brewing. I could vividly hear it becoming more and more heated, then suddenly, bang! A lad in the queue headbutted the bouncer, this lad was then dragged into the club where I'm fairly sure he got a good beating. Fuck this, I'm done! I made a quick exit, left the lads and caught the last bus home. Even though this encounter had shaken me up there was part of me that privately celebrated my victory. I'd pulled the trigger and destroyed someone in a split second. I was now hungry to understand how to control and master that feeling which preceded the strike though, the adrenaline and fear had left me all but completely paralysed and I never wanted to have to go through that, ever again.

Who the fuck was that animal who took charge though? That wasn't me, that isn't who I am. I was a competitive fighter for fuck's sake. I'd compete round after round of skilful sparring and it never felt like this. Why, when faced with real danger, did I forget everything I'd been training for and just lash out? It was now becoming very evident that the confidence I had gained over the years from karate had been built on very dodgy foundations, a devastating storm had shown up and my entire world had begun to crumble.

Chapter #7

Fake

In the opening chapter of this book you were introduced to the world of the bouncer, a profession that serves up violence like McDonald's serves up burgers; fast, regular and often surrounded by fucking idiots. It was important for me to start this book this way because I wanted to trigger your judgment. Thug, animal, and bully will have been a few, but certainly not all of the words that entered your head whilst visualising the brutality that I'd dished out that night. Scared, vulnerable and confused would be a far more accurate account of what was really going on for me though. Being a bouncer wasn't something I'd ever seen myself doing, in fact quite the opposite. The incident on Corporation Street followed by the kick off at the Top Spot was something I never wanted to ever see again, but a chance meeting and a simple comment changed everything. Let's rewind back about a decade from the first chapter.

The City Centre night club in Coventry was the venue for my next karate competition. This event had pretty much every karate club in the city fielding fighters, with two of those fighters being well known and well-respected men from an equally well known and respected Shotokan club. Both men were also bouncers in the very nightclub that we were competing at. They were on their territory, if you like. I was nineteen years of age and rapidly climbing the ranks on the competitive karate circuit. In the lead up I'd viewed this competition as a fairly easy, domestic affair given the calibre of athletes I'd been beating of late. I did indeed pick up the winner's trophy, but the hardware wasn't the only thing I left with that day. After winning my way to the final I sat chatting to a few of the other competitors, all of whom were singing my praises and I of course was lapping it up. I really was becoming that someone I'd craved to be as a child. One of the competitors wasn't quite as complimentary though. "This is just the sport part of karate and you're very good at it, but you wouldn't last a second in a real street fight." This guy was one of the bouncers who incidentally, I'd just beaten in the second round. "Not all roads lead to the street you know, and I am perfectly happy just doing the sport part," I replied. Sore loser! I put it down to him having been beaten whilst his bouncer-colleagues had watched on, he was carrying a bruised ego. I left the venue with the winner's trophy that day but I also carried a bunch of questions that I knew I could no longer ignore.

A few months had now passed when a bloke visited our karate club to get some different sparring experience. Rob was a talented Taekwondo exponent and when I say Taekwondo, I am talking about old-school, proper Taekwondo. He was a good all-rounder who also had a lot of experience as an amateur boxer and now he wanted to test himself in other combat sparring disciplines. He was about ten years older than me, he carried that experience with a confidence that was somewhat intimidating to my teenage mind. I had at this time really picked up my game, not only was I winning tournaments but I was also working on what I called, in my own head at least, 'street' karate. Only I knew what 'street' karate meant. I never really shared those thoughts with anyone at the time but opponents in the club knew that when they sparred with me there was a good chance they would be hit with stuff that was never normally taught or used in the club. When Rob asked for some sparring partners, he was sent over to me as I heard the club instructor say, "Good luck!" I recall Rob smiling and asking, "Was he talking to you or me?" I wasn't sure but it wasn't too long before we both found out.

I now know in hindsight that many of my club mates found me to be a bit of a handful. I was not only very passionate about my training but at the time I was also having an internal battle that I was really struggling with. After the incident on Corporation Street I'd started dropping headbutts, followed by powerful body kicks as finishers in sparring sessions to prove to myself that what I had really worked. This didn't always go down well with some of the other club members, even though I did always try to control the contact and the force I used. Whilst Rob and I had been sparring he'd hit me with a few hooks - one that rocked my head then a side kick that knocked the wind out of me. It was clear that I was going to have to pick up my game and find something to stop him but every time I found something he had an answer for it. His knowledge and experience were winning the day. Well, until I landed a right cross that stunned him and this gave me a clear unguarded opening for a front kick to the body that put him on his knees. He was not going to stay down and even though the wind had been knocked out of him he just got right back up. His legs had a different idea though and refused to move so I grabbed him, dropped the nut to his cheek bone and swept his feet from under him. He hit the floor and just lay there laughing. "Fuck me, have you ever thought about working the door?" It turned out that Rob was a Bouncer in a pub/club just on the outskirts of Coventry. "I think you could be a good addition to the crew we have." My heart sank, here I was once again faced with battling what I can only describe as my own identity crisis. 'I'm an athlete in a fighting sport, not a bouncer and let that be the end of it' but deep down I just couldn't ignore that I was scared to death about street confrontations and yet again felt like I had something to prove. I really didn't want to go there again, it would be a lot easier to just enjoy the skills of competitive fighting but I was, however, still fighting those demons that had made me run out of the classroom all those years ago. Why the fuck is that still haunting me? I had now found something that I excelled at, sport fighting, and I was in danger of it all being taken away courtesy of my own insecurities.

Rob saw me as a real fighter, someone who could take care of themselves, but I saw a fake, a pretender, someone who looked tough and capable but beneath the surface was still that same scared little kid who had always run away. I had to do it; I knew that if I couldn't get past the fear, then this sport that I loved would have to go. Rational thought escaped me, "Yeah, I'm in, let's do it."

As I pondered my future in the karate world, I knew I'd always be surrounded by practitioners who taught self-defence but couldn't walk the walk. They'd speak about their physical skills relating to street encounters, despite having never had a real fight in their life and I wasn't going to become one of those people, those pretenders. Whilst I loved and was proud of what I'd achieved and who I'd become as an athlete, it wasn't enough. I still felt like I had something to prove. Rob had only witnessed my ability in that sparring session and had no idea about the battle I was having with myself mentally. I did tell him initially that I thought of myself as more of an athlete than a real fighter, but then quickly changed course when I heard myself making excuses and basically once again running away. I had indeed lied to the bouncer I'd beaten at the City Centre Club competition. I wasn't happy being good at just the sport. I still had questions and just maybe Rob could help me find some answers.

The club where Rob worked was just on the outskirts of Coventry and had a reputation for violence which he'd told me was greatly exaggerated. My first shift started well with Rob singing my praises to some of the other bouncers which instantly put me under pressure. "You want to see this fucker scrap!" to which someone replied immediately, "Well that shouldn't take long then," and proceeded to reel off some well-known undesirables who were in the club at the time, causing a problem. Rob assured me I needn't worry and that he would go and sort it out, leaving me at the club entrance while he went off to chat with the aforementioned. He'd only been gone for what I thought was a few minutes when I could hear it kicking off inside.

As I made my way through to the bar area, I could see that Rob had already floored one guy and had grabbed another by the throat. It was now a mass brawl and there was no stopping it. Bouncers were outnumbered. Throwing myself into this felt like a suicide mission! I froze momentarily, desperate to turn on my heels and get the hell out of there but I managed to pluck up some courage within a few seconds and headed into the fray. I had zero fucking idea what to do and all I remember was people hurling abuse at each other. Some were throwing glasses while others were trying to fight but were being pulled away by friends or girlfriends. Rob pushed the guy he had by the throat towards me shouting, "Get this cunt out!" I tried to grab him but somehow he broke free from my grip. Another bouncer stepped in and cracked him across the jaw, knocking him clean out. He and Rob then started pushing the others who were involved towards the exit. What was I doing at this point? Well apart from shitting myself, I was doing sweet fuck all. Feeling completely out of my depth, I'd frozen in both mind and body.

The remainder of the night was a blur until I was left on the entrance door alone, only to be confronted by one of the blokes who had been knocked out earlier and then kicked out. His battered and bloodied face appeared at the door and had attempted to saunter past me back into the club. I put my hand on his chest to stop him to which he responded with, "Get your fucking hands off me." At that moment this was enough for my bottle to go and I let him walk in. My legs felt so weak, I literally felt the blood rush away from my face and I must have looked like a ghost. It was at this precise moment that I realised this job had nothing to do with being a good fighter. No, this job required a skill that I didn't have, a skill I thought I was unlikely to ever have.

Going back to the original mass-brawl that evening, it had kicked off because this guy, the one I'd just let back in, had pushed a glass into the face of a woman who had refused his advances and when jumped on by bystanders he smashed a bottle on the bar and was stabbing anyone within his reach. His accomplices had picked up chairs and tables hurling them at the bouncers. These types of kick-offs are fast and they're brutal and I was most certainly out of my depth, I'd mentally lost the battle and could see no way back. This guy was now back in the club and I pretended he'd snuck past without me seeing him.

"He's back in Rob," I shouted over to him, and through sheer fear I let him deal with it, and deal with it he did. Bang! Rob knocked him clean out and then the other bouncers proceeded to stamp and kick his head around like a football. They then dragged him out the back door and just dumped him there. The rest of the night went on without incident and the other bouncers seemed to just shake off what had happened as another day at the office. I went home that night convinced I would be getting a visit from the police. No way was this guy alive; I was sure I had just watched him being kicked to death. My mind was working overtime, I had never seen such brutality and I most certainly didn't understand how it was glossed over like someone had spilt a drink. I phoned Rob the next day and told him some bullshit story about why I couldn't work there anymore and that I quit. Rob just laughed and fortunately didn't give me a hard time over my decision.

My questions had well and truly been answered and now it was time to throw myself into the sport I loved and leave all that other nonsense in the hands of the people who can really do it. The ensuing months had me reliving this dreadful experience over and over. It had taught me a lot and answered many of my questions which then I found myself sharing with my club mates and competitors alike, but what I had to say seemed to be falling on deaf ears. I was nineteen, a kid in many of their eyes so what did I know? I'd been involved in karate for five minutes compared to a decade for some of them. "There was no such thing as sport karate when we started," stated one of them as he made a fist with the middle finger knuckle protruding. "Punch somebody in the eye with this and it's over." "Ribs! Break the ribs! That's what traditional techniques are designed to do," claimed another. I'd shake my head at the naivety and pure ignorance from people who'd never had any kind of confrontation on the street.

Matthew Syed, has a chapter in his book Black Box Thinking, called Scared Straight. He talks about a group of teenagers in the United States, all of whom were petty criminals, car thieves, drug dealers etc. Nothing thus far had steered them away from a life of crime. Seventeen of them, both boys and girls were put on a bus and escorted to Rahway state prison, one of the most notorious detention centres in North America. The visit to Rahway was part of a crime reduction programme, the idea was that giving these youngsters a glimpse of prison life, and what it was really like in a maximum security prison, would shock them into rethinking their behaviour. While on the bus all the teenagers just laughed and joked; they were too tough to be intimidated by anyone, least of all the jailbirds at Rahway. Matthew Syed then goes on to explain, in quite graphic detail, how every one of these teenagers was broken and how on the bus back home one of the kids vomitted, another said, " I'm done with crime, I need to enrol in a college." The visit to Rahway had indeed scared them straight. My first night on the door had had a similar effect, it was my own Rahway. The ruthless reality of violence was scary, the horrendous shift at the nightclub wasn't what I did and who I wanted to be and just like those teenagers, I again found myself needing to rethink my next move.

⋯⊷⊶◈⊷⊶⋯

Chapter #8

It's just a game

Traditional competitive karate is a fast paced, technically skilful game of chess and at the highest level, it's absolutely fascinating to watch. To the casual spectator it can look like two people just bouncing around throwing the occasional punch or kick but to the athlete, the fighter, it's all about employing tricks and setting traps. At international level every fighter has their own game plan, the skill was in figuring it out, making your game plan work better and better each time. It doesn't matter how technically proficient a fighter is, if they don't have tricks and they don't set traps for their opponent to walk into then all they can do is throw kicks and punches and hope they get lucky.

My dream from around the age of seventeen was to be a competitive karate champion, I loved the sport with a passion, spending every waking moment thinking about and preparing for my next competition. I'd done very well thus far, hailing from a small club in Holbrooks Coventry, under the watchful eye of Barry Tatlow and Graham Tucky, the club's instructors. I'd travelled around the country picking up experience and quite a lot of trophies along the way but now it was time for the big one. The alarm sounded and I sat bolt upright. I had hardly slept anyway, seeing every hour on the clock face throughout the longest of nights. It was competition day, the day I had been training intensely for, over the last few months. My 5am alarm was a daily ritual for me now and usually consisted of me dragging myself out of bed, splashing my face with cold water then heading onto the dark, uninviting road for a three-mile jog.

This morning, however, would see me heading to the Crystal Palace Sports Centre in London for the British Karate Championships, the pinnacle of British karate talent and the place to be and perform well if you wanted to pursue an international career. Fast forward a few hours and I would be seen jogging around a huge empty room at the venue and not because I enjoyed jogging, but because I hadn't made the -75 kg weigh-in. I hated jogging with a passion and still do but as the saying goes if you want the rainbow, you have to put up with the rain. My rainbow weighed 2lb and I had just under an hour to lose it. I covered my body with Vaseline and then slipped on a big, black, plastic bin liner. Ten minutes into my jog and I looked like I'd come in from a rainstorm, there was no beautiful rainbow though, only a bright red face and a body soaked in sweat. Another 30 minutes in and I was totally drenched! Jogging for an hour in the end wasn't too difficult for me in those days, it had become part of my daily grind and as all athletes will attest to, it's an essential element for both physical and mental preparation. Having to deliberately drop weight for a particular purpose was a whole new experience for me and one that was going to ultimately steer me in a totally new direction.

I entered the weigh-in room for the second time with quite a bit of trepidation. I was totally convinced I hadn't done enough but to my surprise, after the 60-minute jog, the scale recorded just over a 2lb loss. Sure, it was all water weight but the number on the scale and dropping below 75kg was all that I cared about at that moment in time. I was a karate athlete and had become a champion at many events prior to this, winning domestic tournaments up and down the UK but now, for the first time in my career, I had my sights firmly set on the international scene. Naturally it was the next step for me. I was beginning to look towards international competitions but to do this I had to win my place on the England National Karate Squad. By now, I needed the challenge and the excitement of needing to step things up a gear and strive for that next goal. There was no doubt I had the tools needed to succeed and I was super passionate about my sport, but was I good enough to not only compete against the best, but to beat the best? Well, this was the day and the place to get all of those questions answered.

After the weigh-in I was approached by a very experienced and seasoned international competitor who told me that I'd dropped the 2lb for the second weigh-in wrong and that all I really needed to do in order to lose a measly 2lb was to relax in the sauna for 30-minutes. He went on to say that I'd unnecessarily used fuel, energy which I was going to need later in the day to compete and that my legs were now most probably shot to pieces. Most competitions back in those days were not divided into weight categories but this was the British championships and fielded all the top internationals in the country. If I was going to have any chance at climbing the ranks in this sport I was going to need to learn a lot more about what being a real athlete was all about.

After winning my way through multiple fights I found myself in the semi finals, and had done so by beating some top, talented contenders. I was feeling confident, adrenaline running and felt prepared to take on anyone. I had just one fight left which, if I won, would see me into the British final. In my semi-final I was set to face a very experienced fighter from the legendary Ishinryu Association. Roy Jerome was one of Ticky Donovan's top fighters and Ticky was, at the time, the British coach I was out to impress. Looking back now, the entire match was controversial! The first round had ended in a draw, point-for-point, all the way to the bell. The second round saw the referees and judges booed by the spectators as they awarded Mr. Jerome points which were strongly contested by my coach and the crowd. That too ended in a draw with one of the four corner judges throwing his flag down and calling 'foul' in protest against my techniques not being scored by the referee. This was it now, we were in the third round, 'sudden death' as they used to call it, with the winner being the first person to score a point. I remember us both fighting very cagily, hedging our bets on what the other would do, not wanting to be the person who missed out on making the final. Just one lapse of concentration and it could all be over.

Mr. Jerome certainly had more experience than me, with Ticky on his side-line coaching him. I recall thinking, 'I can't win this, I just can't find my way in and now my legs are cramping!' I noticed that his right guard hand was just a little too low to fully protect his face, giving me a clean shot at landing my left foot, a roundhouse kick, over the top, essentially slapping my instep into his face. It was now or never. In a split second I moved myself into position and I went for it. Boom! As I executed the kick I was hit with a body shot that destroyed me. I'd fallen for it, he set the trap, showed me his face and I'd gone straight for it. As I raised my leg he went straight in for the body punch and it was all over. My knees buckled and down I went, winded and gasping for breath. It was the perfect shot, powerful yet controlled and technically brilliant.

Back then, a body shot which floored the opponent would win you an 'Ippon', a full point, also known as the 'gold standard' of scoring. Ippons were rare for a shot to the body, they were reserved for the creme de la creme so it was no surprise that a fighter like Mr. Jerome was able to pull one out of the bag on such a big occasion and when it counted most. I was beaten by the better man on the day and I tortured myself over not making the weight and consequently burning out too soon.

As I walked away from the area that day I was greeted by complete strangers congratulating me on such a great fight against such an awesome opponent. I'd picked up third place in a competition that had fielded some of the best fighters in Britain and had come so close to taking the title. The next twelve months were filled with a gruelling competitive schedule which had me travelling both domestically and internationally, having now been selected onto the England squad, something I'd trained for and dreamt about for years. My very first international match was England vs. Japan. Wearing an England badge on my Karate Gi had been my goal, my dream and was something that had consumed my focus and attention for the longest time. However, I soon found that I'd never actually thought about what being an international fighter would really mean, winning a European or world title hadn't occurred to me. Yes, I was hungry to travel and represent my country abroad but I soon realised that just the thrill of competing, being on the mat was enough for me and I didn't have the desire to be an international champion.

Unsurprisingly when you are selected ahead of other athletes to represent your country you are selected to win, to dominate at every match, not just to take part. That pressure took away all the fun for me and it became apparent that even going for selection wasn't fair. I felt I may be taking the place of someone who wanted it more than I did so my international career was pretty short, although I can boast about picking up a commonwealth silver before I called it a day.

The next few months saw me replaying that semi-final bout, over and over, something I would often do after a competition, looking for holes in my game. So I'd hardly moved, his positioning was perfect, he'd had me in his sights, like a sniper just waiting to pull the trigger. I'd been taken out by one single shot. As I relived this bout I had a few other flashbacks - Corporation Street, Rob in the nightclub and even the scouse kid on the bus from my school days. They were all over in seconds but the common theme amongst them was to hit first, hit hard and finish it. This was the bit that was missing, the part I hadn't understood. I'd been doing a sport, playing a game, a game with rules and a referee and thought I could take that game into the street and survive. How absurd! It started to dawn on me, I didn't need to become a better fighter; I needed to become good at pulling the trigger, so to speak. If I wanted to be able to do what those bouncers could do then I just needed to get back on the door and give it another shot and that was exactly what I did.

I'd been back on the door for a couple of days when on a particular evening I stood watching a group of unruly lads walking closer and closer towards the entrance. Everything about them screamed trouble, from their body language to the glares, it was obvious there was likely going to be trouble in some form, at some point. Here I was again feeling totally unprepared yet strangely prepared to learn. As the lads got closer, Baz, one of the other bouncers, approached them and told them in a soft and friendly manner that they wouldn't be allowed in. Their collective response was exactly as I'd expected, abusive and threatening. Les and I walked over to Baz who was now surrounded by the group. An altercation can go from zero to full-on kick off in a split second. Bang,

bang, and fucking bang, and a few more for good measure. It was over before it had started. The group had positioned themselves around us, but the other bouncers had been here before and knew the drill. Even though nothing verbally had suggested violence, the body language of the group and their behaviour suggested otherwise and these bouncers weren't going to be caught on the back foot.

All these years I'd been training to be able to fight but what was now dawning on me, was that fighting isn't what happens. A fight happens when two or more people exchange blows and as a bouncer there shouldn't be any exchanges. My colleagues had something I hadn't got, and something I couldn't do at the time. They knew how to control their fear no matter how they felt inside and knew how to knock someone out in the blink of an eye. It was at this moment that it really hit me, if I wanted to be confident in violent situations then I needed to become very good at being violent. Thereafter, a fifteen-year career on the doors of Coventry began.

⸺⸻◆⸻⸺

Chapter #9
Jekyll and Hyde

With over a decade of having now worked in pretty much every pub and nightclub in the city behind me, I'd made many friends and acquired a fair few enemies. I'd seen the best and worst of society and been in situations that made me laugh, cry and some that have had me questioning my own mortality. I've had friends and colleagues pay the ultimate price for second guessing a split-second decision and others who spent many years behind bars because they went a little bit too far. There was a time that I knew and regularly associated with the most violent of violent in Coventry's underworld and was given many opportunities to be part of six figure drug deals. If you work the doors and you know the right people, pretty much anything is possible, the temptations are relentless.

I was not really a bouncer though. I never saw myself as 'one of the lads' or at least I never lived that lifestyle. I was more a Jekyll and Hyde bouncer, my evil ruthless and violent Mr Hyde making brief appearances, but never hanging around long enough to build an entourage. I am not a fighter or a hard man, although the people I have worked the doors with, I know, will beg to differ. I'd just managed to learn how it all worked, get the job done. A hunter doesn't choose to fight with a dangerous grizzly, he just sets a trap and waits for the predator to walk into it, and this was pretty much all I ever did. I set traps.

Working the doors for most bouncers can also be incredibly tedious and boring especially when your shift starts at around 7pm but doesn't start getting busy until around 10pm and this was one of those nights. To kill some time and have a little fun it wasn't uncommon to get involved in some stupid shit. Looking back now, some things we did were really funny while others maybe bordered on bullying, although it didn't feel like that in the moment. The telephone box game was one of those that still makes me cringe a little.

Looking out from the front of the club we had a clear view of four old red phone boxes, the boxes were arranged in a square formation and backed on to each other. This one evening we stood just inside the club's front doors, often using these phone boxes for our entertainment. Gus, the club manager, was always up for a laugh and it was he that instigated this particular evening's events, shall we say? It was the early 90's, nobody had mobile phones, the closest thing to a cordless phone those days was, well, a cordless phone and Gus had one. Not only did he have the phone but also the telephone numbers to each of the four phone boxes.

This evening's entertainment involved ringing one of the phone boxes and waiting for a poor, unsuspecting passer-by to answer and find themselves on the receiving end of Gus's banter. This game was his baby, he was great at it. He dialled the first number and we waited, watching intently like a group of school kids as a chap was just about to pass the boxes. This chap was maybe in his late 60's and looked a little frail but this wasn't going to stop Gus. This chap entered the phone box and lifted the receiver, and Gus said, "Hello, I wonder if you can help me. I'm an engineer with British Telecom and I'm testing the phone boxes." Gus had a very convincing telephone voice. "Yes of course, how can I help?" Gus then proceeded to explain that he wanted him to stand outside of the phone boxes and when he heard one ring, he needed to go in, answer the phone and make sure that the volume in the earpiece was working. "Yes, ok I can do that."

The chap then stood by all four boxes and waited, Gus made one phone ring and the chap approached the box but just as he opened the door Gus would hang up and call the other phone. This chap then made his way to that phone box and once again just as he opened the door Gus would hang up again. He did this repeatedly as we watched this old geezer, dodging between all four boxes but never quite making it on time. We were laughing so hard that he heard us and then realised that he had been duped. I called him over and offered to get him a beer for being such a good sport.

A few minutes had passed when we saw our next victim go into one of the boxes to make a phone call. He was dressed professionally in a suit & tie, looking as though he'd just been to a business meeting or an interview. He was in there a good few minutes as Gus jumped on the opportunity and started one of the other phones ringing and we waited for another passer-by to take the bait. The timing couldn't have been better. A skinhead guy, upon hearing the phone, went in the phone box and picked up the receiver. Gus started, "Hi, I am in the phone box right in front of yours, this is how I meet men. If you are interested in having sex with me just knock on my window." Skinhead guy quickly dropped the receiver, stepped outside and peered into the small, square glass window pane on the side of the booth where the businessman stood, innocently chatting away. The Skinhead guy then went back into his box and picked up the receiver but before he could say anything, Gus continued, "Yes, you just came around and looked at me, do you want to go somewhere for a drink?" The skinhead guy became enraged, stormed out once again, opened the door of this guy's box, grabbing him by his jacket then pulling him out onto the pavement. One minute this guy had been having a nice chat with someone, the next a seemingly-crazy thug is pulling him outside and punching him in the face, that is until we rushed over and pulled the skin head guy off him! Of course, we didn't 'fess up to our silly yet amusing game.

Now with this entertainment over, Derek and I were both standing at the front of the club, chatting and enjoying a pleasant summer evening. The club now had a steady stream of punters arriving, it was a typical Saturday evening and I'd got chatting with someone who was standing a little way down the stairs around ten feet or so away from the front door entrance. We were chatting away when I looked up the steps towards the entrance doors. My heart sank. Eugene, a well-known face from the city was standing at the door. Derek was standing, blocking his path. "Sorry mate, not tonight – you can't come in," to which Eugene replied, "Yeah! And who the fuck is going to stop me?"

This situation was one of many I'd encountered that I would refer to as a triple A threat. The person that we were dealing with here wasn't just a drunk being a little awkward. This was someone involved in organised crime, who wasn't a stranger to prison time and had a reputation for extreme violence with weapons. He had connections, getting on his wrong side would be inviting trouble.

So what do I mean, 'A triple A threat'?

I used this term to describe a person or situation that triggered a release of adrenaline in 3 different waves; Anticipation-Action-Aftermath.

The first wave:

Anticipation: The slow but constant release of adrenaline as you contemplate what is about to happen will make you feel sick; your mouth becomes dry and your heart starts to race and you become anxious.

The second wave:

Action: The release here can come a few different ways. If you become physically engaged in an altercation that lasts minutes you don't really feel the rush of adrenaline that is taking place because you become laser-focused in the moment. As you settle into the task, (fighting) concentration becomes all-consuming but the adrenaline that is rushing through your veins is causing massive amounts of stress and anxiety. If the Action is fast and brutal (one or two seconds) the adrenaline release is massive, making the Action itself, ferocious.

The third wave:

Aftermath: When a very violent altercation is over, (seconds or minutes), the effects related to this rush of adrenaline can last a good while, often leaving you with high blood pressure and panic attacks for some time afterwards. Depending on the type of altercation and the persons involved, you may also be anticipating comebacks which can cause 'the anticipation adrenaline' to kick in again. Comebacks can happen any day at any time thus leaving you in a constant state of anxiety, bad temper, generally on-edge and confrontational. Eugene's presence and demeanour meant all three A's would, essentially, arrive at the same time. Imagine how you'd feel if Ronnie and Reggie Kray had looked you square in the face and asked, "Who the fuck is going to stop me?"

The double doorway entrance was now blocked vertically by Eugene's 6'8" frame and horizontally by his massive outstretched arms, his posture resembling that of Hercules pushing away those massive stone pillars. "Who the fuck is going to stop me?" rang in my ears and a huge dump of adrenaline hit me like a ton of bricks. There was no way Eugene would walk away now, he had a reputation to protect. 'If Derek doesn't knock him out right now, I'm going to have to do it!' This was a very dangerous man and the consequences of him getting in the club were unthinkable. He needed to be gone. I moved closer to the doors expecting Derek to be taking the first shot and putting him to sleep any second, but he was still talking and trying to reason with Eugene.

The window of opportunity to strike first was gone as Eugene, now getting even more aggressive, had taken a step back out of Derek's range. I walked up to the door, my adrenaline racing through my veins. My legs felt heavy, mouth as dry as the Sahara. Using a calm and respectful dialogue, blowing wind up his arse, I recall appealing to his better nature, referencing who he was whilst acknowledging his reputation. "Eugene, please show us a little respect, you know we can't let you in," I spoke, as I approached him, essentially baiting the trap. The anticipation adrenaline was flooding me now and I was in danger of drowning in this tidal wave of fear. I needed to get this over with, I was almost in range. This was no fool though, he knew exactly what I was doing. "Square-go then, is it?" He smiled as he spoke, stepping farther away from the club doors and into a large open space, just next to where the four big red phone boxes stood. As I edged closer, he fired the first shot, his long arm threw a big right cross that I managed to evade pretty easily. I then found myself dodging a flurry of kicks and punches, all of which I either slipped or covered. I remember a hard right fist, meant for my face, hitting my left shoulder and his left hook whizzed past my face. A square-go like this is not like an organised, bare-knuckle boxing match, oh no! Even though those fights are tough, the fighters are overseen by referees who make sure rules are adhered to, just as with a gypsy straightener; there are people around who intervene when necessary. This was no such event though, this was spontaneous, fuelled by instant aggression with ruthless and brutal intentions.

The adrenaline rushing through my veins had now made my legs so heavy to move, in fact amidst the grappling, punching and kicking my legs gave way a few times and I remember falling over as I tried to move away from his punches. We were now in a full-blown scrap in the middle of the town centre with passers by shouting at us to stop, but this was only going to end with someone lying unconscious and that someone wasn't going to be me. You see, if you're knocked out in this kind of fight you get your head jumped on, there's nobody around to save you. These are the types of fights where people get killed.

Eugene started throwing some heavy bombs in the form of kicks. They didn't look very pretty but the few that hit my arms made me very aware about how much power this man had and one wrong move on my part would be catastrophic. I have always been and always will be someone who believes in sound defensive training. If you can't be hit you can't be hurt. Whilst many other fighters concentrate on hitting, I worked hard on not getting hit and in this instance that training was really paying off. This monster of a man hadn't landed anything on me as he'd intended, but I had landed a few nice shots that had resulted in cuts, blood streaming down his face. Derek at this point was in a fight of his own with Eugene's partner in crime who had appeared from nowhere. Eugene was now becoming exhausted and so was I, we'd been fighting for a good few minutes and the adrenaline was taking its toll. He was gasping for breath and had nothing left in the tank, so I capitalised on this and took the opportunity to lunge forward with an almighty head butt which dropped him to his knees, adding a few ferocious punches to his face on his way down. He was now out cold.

The guy that Derek had been fighting with had now legged it. Bouncers from other pubs had come over to help, but it was all over. Eugene lay unconscious, his battered face the only evidence of the violence that had just taken place. After all the shouting and aggression, the silence was now deafening. Passers-by glanced at this person lying on the pavement and simply continued on their way, unaware of what had just taken place. So, what now, is this over? For now, at least it was.

Eugene had been still for maybe a minute then he started to stir, he got to his feet, wiped blood from his nose and mouth, and just stared at me. I really didn't want to be doing this again but it looked like round number two was definitely on the cards. He then clenched his first and put it out for a fist bump. "Respect man." Wait, what?! He'd put his fist out and conceded. I just did likewise, our fists bumped, he walked away seemingly accepting defeat giving me respect for the victory, or at least that's what I thought.

Twenty minutes or so had now passed and my adrenaline was still actively controlling my mood. You don't just have an altercation of that magnitude and then when it's over continue like nothing has happened, the feeling of high alert can stay with you for many hours. Derek and I were still standing outside, going over what had just taken place. I told Derek that I didn't think this was over. I was right. "He's back," says Derek as he points to a figure walking up the ramp that leads from lower Smithford way. Sure enough it was Eugene. As he approached, he pointed at me and shouted, "Another go!" I really wasn't ready for this, I was on the come-down and I wasn't mentally prepared to be doing this again but of course I had no choice. This wasn't going to be another fight though, Eugene, I've got other ideas. He reached into his jacket and pulled out an axe and then dashed towards us. Both Derek and I ran the half-dozen steps back into the club and slammed shut the big wooden entrance doors, Derek then ran to the back entrance to make sure that we had that covered also.

Inevitably, it wasn't too long before the police arrived. You don't pull out an axe in a public place and it goes unnoticed. Eugene was of course arrested and both Derek and I were interviewed. "Axe? Nope, I didn't see an axe, it was a just a little scuffle on the door." The police wanted to put this man away, he had a lot of previous offences but they couldn't nail him. They were hoping our encounter would be the tipping point to locking him up for a long time. As a bouncer, being responsible for putting somebody behind bars is not a reputation you want to carry and there is a code of conduct that all bouncers understand.

A week later a few of Eugene's henchmen showed up at the club's back doors asking for me by name. They hadn't come looking for revenge, all they wanted was for me to meet with Eugene. He was sure that he would be going to jail after this, he just needed reassurance that I wouldn't be showing up at his court date. We arranged to meet in a town centre pub, somewhere public. This wasn't someone to be trusted though so I, for sure, wasn't turning up alone. He of course had the same idea. As I approached the pub a car pulled up alongside me. I turned my head just as the car's passenger window was being lowered. "Hey man, just you and me in there." It was Eugene, he got out and made his way into the pub. The car, with the engine still running and the driver looking like he was ready for a quick getaway, made me nervous.

Maybe I'd watched too many of those mafia movies. Perhaps I was being paranoid or just maybe this wasn't going to be only a chat. My back-up was already inside the pub and I felt sure his would be, too. As I entered the pub I saw that Eugene had already taken a seat at the bar. "So what are you having?" As he spoke he put out his hand, "Thanks for meeting me man, I have really fucked up, I just want this all to go away." We then entered into quite a lengthy conversation about his drug addiction and how he was basically losing the battle. I really couldn't believe what I was hearing, it just sounded like bullshit, he needed me to keep him out of jail. He told me that he'd been so wasted that particular night that he had no recollection of what had transpired. I wasn't going to push this any further, I really wasn't buying it though. I didn't believe or trust him. I felt like he was now baiting a trap for me and the sooner I got out of the pub the better. I told him that he didn't need to worry, that I had no intention of going to court and he should just show me the same respect and not come to the club where I worked, again. He just smiled, shook my hand, then he left. That was it, it was over.

His case never made it to court, although a few weeks later I heard that he was locked up for battering his girlfriend and kids. I spent many sleepless nights over that evening for a long time. When Eugene first came to the club and was turned away, he'd stepped back from the entrance when I spoke to him, calling me out for a square-go. I'd had ample opportunity to just close the door on him. If I had done that then all this shit could have been avoided. The question I was now asking myself was, 'Why the fuck hadn't I?'

Chapter #10

Angus MacGregor

I was sitting in a small, cold room in Manchester, UK in the middle of winter. A man walked in, "Hi my name is Brian and I will be doing your make-up today." He then reached into a cupboard and pulled out a black waistcoat, a tartan kilt and a white sporran. "There you go, see how these fit you." He laughed and said, "You know what you're supposed to wear under a kilt right? Nothing!" He then wandered off giggling, leaving me slightly bewildered as to what I'd let myself in for. I was in Manchester to play the role of Angus MacGregor, a Scottish brawler, in a video game called Kasumi Ninja. They wanted someone with a martial arts background who could also look like a scruffy street fighter, well they had come to the right chap! The irony could not be overstated. I slipped on the waist coat, pulled up my kilt and sat in the makeup chair. Brian glued a big red beard on my face and when the transformation was complete I took a look in the mirror and thought, 'Yeah my mother would be proud.' My mum was born in Scotland and as kids she would often take us to visit relatives in Edinburgh where it's not uncommon for men to venture out wearing traditional Celtic attire. I distinctly remember my grandad saying, "One day we will get the wee bairn his own kilt," so whilst it felt mildly strange to be wearing what was essentially a skirt, I also felt a little nostalgic and warm inside.

Brian handed me a cup of tea and we sat watching one of the other actors finish their takes before I took to the floor. A young lady was doing her moves in front of a green screen.

I really wasn't sure what I was watching though as this lady didn't appear to be demonstrating any particular skill/ability. What was her specialism, I wondered? She was being directed to throw a punch at an imaginary person and then also behave like she had been hit so that the game creators could superimpose other fight characters into the finished game. She was doing as she was asked but in fairness pretty much anyone off the street could have done the same, so my question was, "Well, what do you need me for?" Brian then informed me that it was his understanding that I was the only actual skilled talent that they had hired.

With high expectations, the shoot director came over and asked me what I had in store for them. "No pressure, but we can't wait to see what you're going to do for us!" "Wait what?" I replied. "So you don't have any scripted fight choreography planned for my character?" "Well no, not really, we just see Angus as a burly, butch, brawler. You have martial arts experience and you're a nightclub bouncer so I'm sure between us we can come up with something, right?" My brain started ticking over and thoughts came flooding in, not about the video game though but about what Brian had said. 'It was my understanding that you were the only actual skilled talent that they had hired.' It had never registered before, I actually had skills, talents that could be used in so many different ways! That particular day however, those skills were needed for a video game, but tomorrow, what about tomorrow? I started to look at all of my knowledge and experiences and where they could be utilised. I became super excited about the possibilities, but for now I just needed to concentrate on Angus and get creative.

"Maybe he lifts his kilt and shoots a fireball from his crotch?" "Brilliant!" they said. "What about Angus's final death move?" "Ok, how about I throw a punch combination,

I spin around, kick the head clean off their shoulders into the air, then as the head comes back down, I head butt it, look at the camera and shout 'Och Aye'?" My inventive imagination never lets me down. Angus' death move was a big hit in the studio, the crew loved it and I have to say we had some great fun filming those scenes. The game was released about a year later and got terrible reviews mainly because the game was, in fact, terrible! My character, however, was widely reported as the star of the show and started to gain something of a cult following, mainly due to a few crazy moves that you would never have expected to see in a video game at that time. Who would have imagined that many years later you would be able to go to something called YouTube, type in Kasumi Ninja Angus and be able to see my character. Yes, do it now!

I'd travelled to Manchester that day as a former, competitive karate athlete and a former, nightclub bouncer. I use the word former because although I was still physically active at both, I'd mentally begun my retirement in both. But how do you retire from who you are and what you do, how do you make that breakaway and what do you breakaway, to? Brian's comment, still ringing in my ears, had given me the answer. I had skills and as I drove south on the M6 I began unravelling them in my mind's eye. 'As a karate athlete I am, by default, very knowledgeable in physical exercise, so I go on some training courses and become a fitness coach. I've been lifting weights for many years, so do the certification and become personal trainer. As a bouncer, I understood how to deal with very real and very violent situations, there's going to be a market for that knowledge surely?' Once I learned how to diversify my own thinking, the list of possibilities just kept coming.

While driving home I inevitably ran into a traffic jam and found myself bumper to bumper for what seemed like an eternity with just the occasional glimmer of hope when the car in front moved about a foot. When cars did start to move I passed a 'Lane Closed Ahead' sign indicating that we should be looking to change lanes as soon as possible. I indicated my intention and was promptly let in by the car to my right. Now with the traffic crawling along slowly (crawling's always better than not moving at all), I see another 'Lane Closed Ahead' sign indicating, once again, that we should all be looking to move over whenever possible. You get the drift. I'd now been stuck in traffic for over two hours and travelled maybe twenty miles. My head was a bit mashed in anyway but seeing other cars totally ignoring the signs and just driving to the front of the queue, forcing their way in, triggered the fight or flight adrenaline. My heart began to race. 'Who the fuck do they think they are? I've been waiting in this queue for hours, the cheeky impatient wankers. They have no idea what I could do to them.'

I paused, hearing myself; being so fucking arrogant and righteous had me deeply disturbed. Who the fuck had I become or at least who was I becoming? I'd learned how to face a confrontation, read the situation and pull the trigger, but then I thought about the fight with Eugene. 'Why didn't I just close the doors?' I'd wanted to be someone but the someone I became at times was a person I didn't recognise or even a person I liked. That had to change. I needed to have a good chat with myself and it went something like this. 'I created you (the protector in me) to be strong, to be confident and to be violent when violence was necessary. I didn't create you to cause trouble when trouble could be avoided. I've allowed you to become too strong and too powerful, I think maybe it's time for you to take a back seat now.' It was becoming clear that this alter ego who I'd created to deal with all the shit in my life, had developed an ego all of his own. He needed to know this wasn't acceptable.

I sat back in my car seat, turned the radio up and just let everyone get on with whatever they were doing. As the minutes passed so did the rage. I sat and watched as complete strangers drove past me, cut to the front of the queue and after a few minutes they were gone. I sat calmly, listening to the radio, smiling to myself. I didn't know these people. I am not the stay-in-your-lane police and to move my car into a position to stop them, straddling both lanes to block any one passing would have had absolutely no positive outcome. Why do I need to create a road rage incident with people I don't know, will never see again and more importantly drivers who will be gone in, literally, seconds? The rest of the drive had me feeling like a massive weight having taken off my shoulders, like I had offloaded a massive amount of baggage. I woke up the next morning feeling like a nobody, I know that sounds strange, but I felt almost reborn, naked, vulnerable, yet strangely it felt amazing. I had what I can only really describe as a spiritual awakening, a call to higher consciousness with a deeper mental awareness. Being someone, even in just my own head, had made me feel like I'd had something to prove all the fucking time and it had been really wearing me down.

Today, I find myself looking at so many people who are still doing what they've been doing most of their life and I often ask myself this question: are they doing what they do because they are truly happy with their life, or because they've never found the courage to become a nobody again and start over? I am not judging anybody, I'm just observing and wondering. As a bouncer I would very often find myself talking about violence. When I talked about violence, trained for violence and associated with violent people the universe assumed I wanted violence in my life so it gave me it in abundance. As a child I wanted to be someone, I became that someone by being respected in the world of competitive karate and by the men I stood beside on the front line of violence on a nightclub door, but now I realised that I was so much more than both of these things. And having now recognised that I'd been giving certain emotions (alter egos) too much nourishment, it was time for a change, it was time for me to reinvent myself.

"As far as I'm aware, you are the only skilled talent that we have hired," Brian had really got me thinking. I hadn't walked onto that studio floor because I was good at karate or because I was a tough nightclub bouncer, oh no. The only thing that had got me through those doors was confidence and it was really only confidence that I had sought all along anyway. It had come to my attention that lots of people who were far more capable than myself had been offered the part of Angus but had declined, saying that they thought the game would make them look stupid. I was the only one who saw a positive instead of a negative. As Richard Branson said, 'If somebody offers you an amazing opportunity but you are not sure you can do it, say yes – then learn how to do it later!' I'd no idea what this game was about or if I could even give them what they wanted, but I'd gained the confidence which allowed me to attack life and not worry about failing. In fact, I'd began embracing failure, framing it as a learning curve. 'You miss 100% of the shots you don't take.' (Wayne Gretzky, Ice Hockey legend).

What was really dawning on me after this video game shoot was that I did indeed have so many options that had never even occurred to me before. Door work was how I fed my protector ego and it was working the doors that built my confidence. Running karate clubs was how I fed my artistic ego. It was an outlet that allowed me to be creative and to show off my talent. It was now time for both karate and door work to take a back seat though and for me to focus on new adventures and the alter egos they would reveal in me.

Chapter #11

Sliding Doors

A lady gets to the tube station and rushes to the platform only to find that she is, literally, seconds too late. The train doors close and she's left standing there on the platform. If only she hadn't had that last cup of coffee or stood chatting with a friend, she would have made it onto the train. Now she's going to miss that important meeting and there's nothing she can do about it. She heads back home, walks through her front door and hears people talking upstairs. She goes up only to find her husband in bed with another woman and her world begins to fall apart. Sliding Doors is a movie starring Gwyneth Paltrow and follows a woman whose life is looked at from two different perspectives and demonstrates how one small life event can change everything else. In the movie the scene is replayed, this time she makes it onto the train and now two different lives begin to play out. Accepting that the difficult, somewhat shit things that had happened to me in my life so far were in fact positive things was part of my spiritual awakening. Even going back to when I ran out of the school classroom, embarrassed and angry. At the time it was horrendous but the path it forced me down was exactly the path I was required to take and had started to shape me as a young man.

It was 1988. I'd taken the train from Coventry down to Crystal Palace Sports Centre in London. The train was delayed so I was running about an hour late. I was travelling to the England Karate squad training and to try-out for the European Championships team and individual selection.

This was a momentous event in the karate calendar, the crème de la crème of English competitors would be there, all fighting for a coveted spot on the team to travel abroad and represent their country. It was something I'd been training on for months.

I eventually arrived at the venue, panicked and rushed, two hours later than the start time. Even though the event's training sessions had only just started and the place selections weren't happening until early evening, that didn't matter. The British Coach, Ticky Donovan, told me I was late so I couldn't participate. I couldn't believe my ears, I was gutted. I explained that the train had been delayed and it wasn't my fault. Ticky was having none of it, "The people who live the farthest away should always be the people who arrive first." I was angry and upset, my late arrival wasn't my fault and I was being penalised for something which was outside of my control. It didn't sit well with me and I was confused about the 'people who live farthest away should always arrive first' comment. Ticky continued, "Failure to prepare is preparing to fail and if you are serious about your international competitive career then you need to understand there are no excuses." The reason I should have been at the venue first was because I should have travelled down the night before, got a hotel close to the venue and even had a taxi booked from the hotel with time to spare. At that time I didn't agree. Ticky continued, "If you were selected for the European championships in Vienna, what day would you be travelling, the morning of the competition or days before?" Of course he was right and in hindsight this was a big lesson for me. I was always a good time keeper and thought I understood the importance of good preparation but I hadn't, until this point, been prepared for other people's fuck ups and I guess at the time I hadn't even thought about it.

Like everyone does I have had those occasions where I've said, if only I had made this choice instead of that choice, or, if I had been there just a little bit later or just a little bit earlier, what would have happened? Just like the lady who missed her train, my future was going to play out the way it was meant to. The squad that was picked and eventually travelled to Vienna were there for a week, so what was I doing during that week? I don't remember now, all these years later, but whatever it was, it created other paths, opened and closed other doors. Doors that wouldn't have been shown to me had I been in Vienna. My point here is had I been selected and gone to the European Championships my entire life would have taken a different path, not unlike the contestants on talent-spotting TV shows, like the X-Factor or American Idol. It's rarely the winner who goes on to be crazy-successful. Jennifer Hudson took seventh place on American Idol; One Direction took third place on the X-Factor and Lewis Capaldi never even got a call back from Britain's Got Talent. They all went on to build amazing careers despite what they may well have viewed as a failure at the time.

I'd often replayed my past competition bouts and beaten myself up thinking about the mistakes I'd made. 'If I'd only just stuck to the basics! Why did I try and sweep when I just needed a basic punch to win that round? Not winning that competition meant not getting press coverage. Not having press coverage meant I wasn't going to be getting free publicity for my clubs etc. The negatives associated with failure don't really exist though because as the saying goes, every cloud has a silver lining. I had now for some reason started to look closer at the knock-on effect of both action and inaction, success and failure, and to quote another classic, 'Turn a different corner and we never would have met.'

Going back to an event when I worked the door in Coventry one evening, the club manager asked me to go and speak to a guy who'd been standing outside the ladies' toilets and charging them to go in. The guy in question was a lean, muscular looking chap with a tattooed neck and short, cropped hair. He looked like a proper gym regular and seemed 'clued-in'. I approached and told him he needed to leave the club whilst positioning myself for his response. He just laughed. "Busted!" he said and began walking to the exit. He headed towards the door and just as he was about to step outside he said in a very loud voice, "Me and you, square-go". He then went on to brag about how his full-time job was as a sparring partner for all of Coventry's pro boxers and he started dropping names of their financial backers, basically all the criminals of Coventry's underworld. "I get paid a grand a day to keep these champs sharp and ready to fight," he said, squaring up to me, only to be hit by my left hook that put him to sleep the second it landed.

He had no sooner hit the deck when I felt something hit me on the top of my head and the weight of someone who had jumped on my back. I felt blood dripping down the front of my face, this guy's girlfriend had hit me on the head with the heel of her shoe before jumping on my back and attempting to get me into a rear chokehold. Her arm around my throat, I quickly and forcefully bent over, effectively throwing her over my shoulder and her body hit the tarmac with a thud. The boyfriend was now back on his feet, shouting about how the boys would be coming down to sort me out because he wouldn't be allowed to spar with them now that he'd suffered a brain 'trauma'. They'd no longer be able to compete so their financial backers would be losing millions. It was all my fault apparently! He approached me once more and squared up to me. I knocked him out again and he hit the deck. After a moment of watching to make sure he was coming round again, the other doorman and I closed the front door and we left them out there to pick themselves up and move on. Nine times out of ten, you close the door on this type of troublemaker and they disappear onto the next venue of their own accord. We looked through the door's spyhole a few minutes later and they'd seemingly left.

About fifteen minutes had passed and we suddenly heard the sound of sirens outside of the club. We opened the door to see a fire engine and a few police cars. On speaking to the old bill it became clear that someone had called 999 saying that there was a fire at the club. A fire, where? Upon realising this was a hoax call the police quickly determined that the 999 call had been made from the phone box located just next to the club and to my shock and disbelief, was still occupied by... you guessed it, Mr Sparring Partner. He'd not only made the hoax call, he also actually stayed in the phone box to watch it all unfold. As the police approached and opened the door, they quickly began to arrest him. "You don't know who you're fucking with, I'm a professional sparring partner for all the Coventry Pro boxers...I get paid a grand a day," blah blah blah. The look on the policemen's faces was priceless.

We joked about this guy and the evening's antics for a good while after, but we also chatted about how bad it could have been for me if the girlfriend had used a blade or a broken glass, instead of just the heel of her shoe. These conversations and reflections had started to become a regular thing for me now, following incidents on the door and I'd now begun second guessing my intentions and asking myself, 'What if?' I'd spent many years growing my confidence and capability, only to realise that I'd become dangerous, yet still vulnerable. Vulnerable to the decisions, moods and mental state of complete strangers who were often alcohol and drug-fuelled. I'd begun to feel like I was putting my life and liberty into someone else's hands at the start of each shift, so much so that I decided it was time to start working less and less shifts with the ultimate goal of quitting door work altogether.

Fast forward a few months and I was turning down the odd shift here and there which I previously would have worked in a heartbeat. I'd of course now begun thinking about new ventures, possibilities of what I wanted the future to look like. I just needed to make the decision and quit the door work all together, but I wasn't quite there yet.

It was a quiet midweek night in a local pub where I'd been the head bouncer for a good while. I knew pretty much all of the regulars and had earned their respect. That being said, the respect they had for me didn't get in the way of the loyalty they had for their friends and when it kicks off, all of that respect can fly out of the window or in this particular instance, hide in the toilets. I'd arrived early for work that evening, so early that no other bouncers had got there yet. I hadn't been in the pub long when I was approached by the manager who informed me that RB had just been released from jail and the word on the street was that he was on a local pub crawl.

A sense of dread flooded my veins. I'd never had any contact with RB but I'd heard his name mentioned many times. He wasn't a hard man or even somebody who could have a decent scrap but he was bad news. A petty criminal who lived his life in a revolving door that has seen him in and out of jail from a very early age and like most troublemakers, he was really just a coward who had something to prove to himself. A glass in the face or knife in the back was his modus operandi, his way of 'doing business'. So, despite his lack of fighting ability, he was very dangerous nonetheless. I was told that it was more than likely he'd be attempting to come into the pub with a group of his co-conspirators so I needed to be on the ball. Well, that's all fine and dandy coming from the manager, but I had no fucking idea what he even looked like!

A few of the regulars standing nearby knew who RB was and on hearing that he may make an appearance became very vocal about how they would 'deal with him' if he showed his face. Great! That saves me a job then! They'd no sooner declared themselves the saloon sheriffs when the RB did indeed make an appearance just as some of them made a swift disappearance... to the nearby toilets. Like I said, I had no idea what RB looked like, I'd just heard somebody say, "He's here," as a group of Neanderthals sauntered in the front door. "So, which one is he?" My question was totally ignored as even more of the regulars moved away from the bar, wanting to disassociate themselves from any RB-related conversation. I looked around for the pub manager but even he'd gone AWOL. I walked over to the group and calmly asked, "Which one of you is RB?" Safe to say I was shitting myself inside but I wasn't about to let anyone else sense that. They looked at me confidently then turned away. I asked again, "Lads, which one of you is RB?" "I am," came a voice from the bar, he turned and looked at me. "We need to have a chat." I nodded my head indicating that he should follow me and then, "I am," came a second voice from behind me. "I am RB," came another voice to my right. I paused for a few seconds, very aware that I was on my own and in grave danger of getting a good kicking. "Ok, I guess you're all barred then." I made my way to the end of the bar and just gave them space, the other bouncers would be here soon but I'd already lit the fuse and if this bomb goes off now, I am fucked given there was about eight of them.

As I watched them and waited for the other bouncers to show up one of the lads in the group came over to me, "I'm RB, I know who you are, I don't want to make an enemy of you." He went on to say he was just out of jail and wanted to make a clean start and that when they'd finished their drinks they would all leave. We spoke for a few minutes and it became abundantly clear that this guy was never going to change, he was seemingly a drug addict and I'd heard he was a functioning alcoholic. He was sober and calm during our conversation but I could see his demons in his eyes. He explained that he'd been in prison with a few lads who knew and respected me, so he'd show me the same respect and leave. The truth was he had no respect for anything or anyone, the Chinese whispers and exaggerations spouted by inmates had him believing that I was dangerous and not to be fucked with. This is not a bad reputation to have as it can often, such as in this case, save you from problems. In other situations it can also make you a target for those looking to build their own reputation.

True to his word RB and his crew did drink up and left the pub but my dealings with him were only delayed. He showed up at another venue just a few months later. A DJ friend of mine had set up some midweek parties at a local working men's club in Coventry and asked if I would provide the bouncers, so a few lads and I worked these events once a week. There was never any trouble given the type of people these events catered for were more of an older, laidback type. I was standing at the entrance when RB showed up with a friend. At first I wasn't going to let him in but he seemed stone cold sober and I was pleasantly surprised to see that he was behaving like a real gentleman, for a change.

I told him, "Any trouble and you're gone." He laughed. "I know better than to fuck with you," he replied. He did, of course, fuck up and I had to ask him to leave a few hours later for being confrontational with other punters. He complied and left of his own accord without too much encouragement from me. I watched him walk out of the club and I thought that my problem with him was over, but then he turned and walked back towards the front door. His eyes glaring, transfixed on me and a facial expression that could only be described as demonic. He then did what anyone who is going to throw a punch does, he so obviously lined me up right before my own eyes. Really? He may as well have just told me what he was thinking. Bang! My right cross landed on his jaw and he landed on his arse, then staggering back to his feet only to be met by my foot in the ribs and he was down again. After lots of groaning and spending half a minute getting his bearings, he got up again and staggered in his drunken state to his car and got in. Surely he wasn't driving away? The stench of alcohol on his breath had been overpowering yet here he was, about to put every motorist in the nearby streets in serious danger. He pulled away, banging into a couple of parked cars as he attempted to navigate the car park like bumper cars at the local fair.

This was now the third time that I'd landed a clean shot on someone without an absolute intention. Previously, when someone told me in their body language that they were going to hit me I'd visualise the sound of my fist connecting with the jawbone. I'd literally be able to taste blood as my mind's eye pictured a face battered and swollen from repeated blows, each one intended to remove the threat to my own safety. I'd become a very dangerous person. The adrenaline that rushed through my veins when violence came calling had made me faster, tougher and ruthless. Now, that same adrenaline was putting the brakes on as I contemplated and, quite frankly, feared the consequences of my actions. I'd always anticipated the consequences of my actions before but usually it was about inaction. The consequences of letting someone take the first shot could mean me lying unconscious and my head being jumped on, like I'd witnessed so many times in my years of working nightclub doors. My inability to pull the trigger with ruthless intentions was now becoming a liability, I was a danger to myself so the sooner I quit this job the better.

RB left the premises that night and I personally never had any contact with him again. I'd often hear his name on the grapevine however as his behaviour never changed and it was many years later, whilst drunk and drugged up, he sped out of a Coventry pub car park one lunch time, driving into two small children, killing them both. His lengthy prison sentence came to an abrupt end when his body was discovered in his cell due to an apparent drug overdose. How the fuck do you OD in jail? Tragically, the father of the two boys subsequently took his own life. To this day I still have the occasional nightmare and panic attack where I question myself, 'What if I'd hit him with absolute intention that night, just like I'd done so many times before and ended RB's life? Would those poor kids still be alive today?' Rational thinking sometimes has a way of evading you when such emotions are involved, but this is what the job can do to you. You simply cannot live a life surrounded by violence and violent people, without it taking its toll.

As you can imagine, with all my real-life door work experience and competitive fighting I'm often asked for advice on self-defence and what would be the best thing for a beginner to learn. My answer will always be the same. Firstly, you need people skills not fighting skills. Being able to control and diffuse a situation with dialogue should always be your primary goal. Those people skills will then let you read where the situation is heading. If you see violence on the cards and you have the option to leave, then take that option. If there is no chance to escape, use dialogue to get into position then quickly put your threat to sleep. Yes, it's very risky but when you have explored every other option to no avail, what are you left with?

One evening, just as the club was closing at 2am, we received a phone call from the chip shop situated next door. The staff were getting some serious grief from a couple of customers and had rung to ask if we, the doormen, could go and help them out. The chippy was literally just around the corner. It was always jam-packed this time of night, owing to the fact this was the only chippy open so late, feeding the hungry revellers as they made their way home. We agreed to pop around and help where we could.

On entering, it was clear the lads causing trouble were very drunk and in high spirits. Initially I gave them the benefit of the doubt, they were just being silly and having some banter with the staff, right? Wrong, one of the lads had taken his order of food and flatly refused to pay. He and his mate were waiting for their second order to be dished up and handed over. The staff quite rightly were refusing to serve him until the first order had been paid for and the situation was becoming more and more heated by the second.

I'd gone to the chippy with two other doormen from the club. Both were stood just behind me as we began to deal with the situation. I confronted food thief number one, a towering 6'3" in height and a minimum of 17 stone in weight (240lbs). He was one hell of a unit. As he arrogantly leaned up against the fruit machine I asked, "So you're not paying for that food then?" "What the fuck does that have to do with you?" came his reply. In all fairness he was right, it had nothing to do with me. It wasn't my chippy and I didn't work there, but I was simply unable to walk away and turn a blind eye by this point. If you're walking along the street and you see someone being attacked, do you intervene or just ignore it? The other guy, who was arguing with the staff at this point, turned and looked at me. Blue Shirt, as we'll call him, had been in the club earlier that evening, I recognised his face. The staff were still refusing to serve him so he reached over and took a handful of chips from fruit machine guy. "I can't make you pay," I said, smiling and turning to Blue Shirt. "But I can stop you coming into the club next time you're on a night out." I'd just thrown down the gauntlet and was waiting for his response. My hope was that this would be enough to show the chippy staff that we'd come to help and we'd tried, but I really wasn't comfortable with the situation. Their sheer arrogance and demeanour screamed 'bully'. My heart was racing. The shop was packed full of people who were now zoned into what was unfolding. The other bouncers and I were now in a very volatile predicament. Fruit Machine guy took a handful of chips and stuffed them in his mouth, "Free food mate!" he said, laughing directly at me.

I looked at my two colleagues, nodded my head indicating it was time for us to leave. Fruit Machine guy had other ideas though. He started to position himself to fire a shot at me, "So what are you going to do now?" He spoke very confidently as he stood away from the fruit machine and stared right into my eyes. He was a few inches taller than me and a lot heavier. His posture and dialogue told me everything I needed to know. Bang. A perfect, clean right cross landed on his jaw. His legs buckled beneath him as he fell back against the fruit machine and onto the chippy floor where he lay unconscious.

The chippy erupted with people pushing and shoving, a mixture of some drunken people celebrating what had just happened and some people completely panicked and desperate to leave. We had no idea who Blue Shirt and Fruit Machine guy were with, or if they were with anyone else at all. Blue Shirt, having seen his mate just knocked out, lunged towards me but there were people in the way and in just a matter of seconds I found myself outside the shop door. He followed, running towards me and straight onto my right cross, immediately followed by a front leg roundhouse kick to his face. My steel toe-capped shoes collided with his jaw, his legs already buckled from the punch. The kick, a split second later, was connecting with a head that was already unconscious. I still remember that I'd even managed to sweep his feet from under him before his unconscious body had a chance to hit the ground.

I can be a dangerous person. Not because I can punch, kick, sweep and head butt with accuracy and power. I'm dangerous because when I am put in this type of situation I see a mental image of the carnage about to happen and I stand and visualise an absolute intention. I'm dangerous because my intention in such a situation is to destroy and eliminate a threat as quickly as possible. This kick-off was in a chippy, but it could have happened on the street, in a pub or pretty much anywhere. I'm dangerous because I can and I will do extreme violence if I feel it is required. Being able to hurt people had made me a danger to myself though. Both, the Fruit Machine guy and Blue Shirt, took a while to get to their feet after the altercation which made me panic. When they did eventually stand up they staggered and fell a few times.

I'd heard many stories about brain bleeds and concussions resulting in death only hours after this type of altercation and I was very aware that my luck may be running out. I'd become worried about my liberty and was convinced it was only a matter of time before I did kill someone. For some reason this particular night made me take a good hard look at the 'what ifs'. I'd been in this type of situation many times before but maybe next time those sliding doors could see me heading to a prison cell or even a mortuary.

Chapter #12

Damaged

"Hey Dave, he's back! I'm sure I just saw his car go by." Dave and I stepped outside the club entrance and stood on the top step which led to a huge, gravelled car park. It was early on a Friday night and the car park was empty. The night club was part of a hotel just on the outskirts of Coventry. Because of its location it attracted punters from nearby Bedworth, Nuneaton, Atherstone and Coventry. We'd kicked a guy out of the club an hour earlier, after which he stood in the car park hurling abuse and threatening to come back and kill us both. Every bouncer knows how it works, they make threats from a safe distance and then you never see them again. Occasionally some people do return and when they do, they come back with a vengeance. This turned out to be one of those times.

Standing at the club entrance, we both watched a car drive past the club, stop, turn around in a side road and drive back towards us. It was indeed the guy that had been kicked out and he was now parked right outside the club. His windows were up and he was just staring at us. Dave wasn't someone to fuck around with and if you're going to make threats you better make good on those threats because Dave will remember you and your day will come. So instead of just ignoring this guy Dave started calling him out, telling him to get out of the car and come have a square-go. To make the situation even worse Dave started laughing at the guy. This enraged him even more and he began wheel spinning, kicking up gravel as his car began doing donuts in the centre of the car park. We just stood there watching from the door, then his car stopped. He got out and reached into the back seat for something. He was too far away for us to see what it was. With the car parked side on to the club doors this guy stood behind the car and positioned himself at the driver's side. We soon realised that what he had in his hand was a crossbow, a full-on, crossbow! He then loaded an arrow and took aim. We quickly legged it inside. Desperate to make sure no one got hurt, Dave ran to one of the side exits to look for an opportunity to come at him from behind while I stayed just inside the front door to watch what he was doing.

As I watched, customers started to arrive in the car park and make their way to the now-closed entrance door. I remember thinking, 'Someone's going to get seriously hurt tonight, with a bloody crossbow of all things!' Before long he got back into his car, sped away and just like that, it was over. One minute we were facing a possible arrow in the head, the next we were talking to a police woman about something I never thought I'd hear anyone say.

Now, with 'William Tell' gone, we were onto our next incident. Two police officers came in looking for a young lady. The lady in question was the ex-girlfriend of a guy we had asked to leave the club, a little earlier. They'd had a bust-up and he'd been getting rowdy and abusive with her. The policewoman was fighting back tears and shaking as she spoke. She told me that they had been to the ex-girlfriend's flat after someone had called the police due to a disturbance. Upon arriving at the flat, the police found the front door had been kicked in and a trail of blood led them to a dismembered puppy. It appeared that this psycho we'd ejected earlier had broken into her flat and chopped up her poor dog.

A bouncer puts himself/herself on the front line of unimaginable violence every time they work a shift and some things just never make any sense. What sort of person gets kicked out of a club, goes home and gets in their car drunk and returns to the club with a crossbow maybe with the real intention of killing someone? How sick do you have to be to chop up a live puppy just to get back at an ex? The physical violence that comes with being a bouncer is only a very small part of the story, the mental battles that a bouncer has to deal with are very often overlooked and in most cases totally ignored. Of course, a bouncer isn't physically fighting with someone every shift they work, but they can, and do find themselves dealing with very high bouts of stress just by watching how other people behave.

One such example that was a real mind fuck made me realise that even otherwise normal people do have a breaking point and behave irrationally. I'd been walking around the club chatting with the customers when amidst the contrast of a dark club and flashing lights, I happened to notice something sparkle in the distance. My attention was drawn to it as I stood on the upper level looking down at the crowd below. Right at the edge of the dance floor was a woman; the sparkling was coming from something she was holding in her right hand. Every few seconds when the disco lights hit the object it reflected the light. I walked down to the ground level and towards her to get a closer look. Was I being paranoid? Was this reflection just from a diamond ring or was there something a little more sinister going on? As I got closer to her I could see she was very upset, distraught, her eyes transfixed on somebody on the dance floor and her face wet with tears. She was holding a heavy beer tumbler, the type that has those tiny window panes and a thick, chunky handle. Well, the windows were no more, the glass had been broken and all that was left was the handle and a long, jagged piece of glass on one end. I've broken up numerous fights over the years where someone's been glassed in the face or bottled around their head; the injuries can be horrendously life changing. I had no choice but to intervene and try to diffuse the situation before some poor, unsuspecting punter's world caved in.

I approached her from the side, slipping my arm around her waist in an attempt to block the hand which held the broken glass, effectively disarming her. "I'm gonna slash her fuckin face up!" she said through the tears. The glass fell from her hand onto the floor, the relief was immense. Upon talking to her I discovered she'd come to the club knowing her husband was there with another woman. She told me that she had no intention of stabbing her husband, she wanted to disfigure the face of the lady he was with.

I have no doubt that I have suffered mentally due to being a bouncer. I've physically survived but the mental damage has left wounds that will never completely heal. I know that many of my fellow bouncers also encounter some degree of Post-Traumatic Stress Disorder (PTSD), something that is typically associated with soldiers returning from war. The amount of stress a bouncer deals with just can't be understated and it triggers whether you're directly involved in an incident, or not. Seeing a young lady holding a weapon that was intended to disfigure someone's face, a lady who turned out to be an innocent party in the end, has a way of triggering an emotion which makes you question your own sanity. To accept that this is a world where someone out there will hurt or even kill someone, any of our loved ones, based purely on a misguidance is very troubling. This young lady could have been anyone's daughter who just happened to say 'yes' when invited to dance and if I hadn't intervened, she would have had her face carved up.

Another young man wasn't quite as lucky. A guy came into the club one evening and asked for a favour. "I don't want to come in but is there any chance you could ask the DJ to put a call out for someone?" This was the mid-eighties, no one had mobile phones so sending a text message to someone wasn't a thing. It was a normal practice to have the DJ make this type of announcement. The guy in front of me looked totally harmless. He wasn't dressed to go into the club, he really just wanted his friend to come out to him. 'No Harm', I thought. The DJ made the announcement and a young lad came out of the club into the reception area. "Someone looking for me?" he asked. I told him that a guy had asked for him and he was waiting outside. This lad had literally just stepped outside, the doors closed behind him when, Bang! A spiked knuckle duster was slammed into his face. He dropped onto the steps, unconscious, before the three of us rushed out to help him. As we did, the guy with the duster started to stamp on his unconscious head. After a quick scuffle I managed to get this guy in a head lock and put him to sleep with a choke, potentially saving the poor lad's life.

These types of what I call 'micro-incidents' are a regular occurrence but like I have said, they are not a direct challenge on the bouncer themselves and each one in isolation can feel like nothing, a non- event, but over time these types of stress-inducing incidents can really take their toll. 'Death by a thousand cuts' is the perfect way to describe it.

It's often the things we don't talk about which cause the most problems for us mentally. You know, those memories that we pushed to the back of our minds because to face them would cause anguish that we really don't want to deal with. Subconsciously we choose to ignore our realities at times and most bouncers I've known over the years would never talk about their anxiety or depression. The perception is, this could be seen as them being 'soft' and not living up to a hardman image they'd worked hard for all those years. But we ignore these symptoms at our peril because they cause greater mental harm by not acknowledging or accepting them.

Whilst writing this book I've had cause to revisit memories that I'd never wanted to ever think about again because of the mental anguish they invoked. I hated what I had to do as a bouncer but when one memory is revisited it opens a door to another and another and another. Even now I've found myself jogging on the treadmill during my morning workouts, sweat mixed with tears pouring down my face as a sea of emotion engulfs me and at times has threatened to destroy me. Recalling encounters, the memories of the people I've had to hurt and the ones who've tried to hurt me, my brain doesn't deliver these memories to my consciousness at one time, enabling me to rationally justify each one. Oh no, the violence, the fear and the lifestyle associated with every encounter arrives like a massive fucking weight that just seems to want to crush me. All of those emotions that I'd either put to rest, tucked away or just plain old ignored have to go somewhere and during a sweaty workout I'd often just let those emotions go, succumbing to the moment.

I think I'm probably one of the lucky ones though. Angus McGregor had saved me, or at least Brian the make-up guy had. After leaving door work I found myself looking towards the fitness industry as my next venture. I didn't know in what capacity just yet but I knew this direction felt right. It was an obvious move, really, given my athletic background. I guess I'd never truly appreciated how a proper workout can release those pent-up emotions and make a massive difference when battling anxiety and depression. Not only were these workouts helping me, but I knew that I now wanted to find a path that would also allow me to help other people.

A bell cannot be unrung and there are things that will never totally go away, things that time will never heel. In my quest to become someone I made many mistakes. As I've already said, I'd believed that becoming a good fighter was the way to be respected and admired, but respected by whom, though? I really hadn't thought that one out. As a competitive fighter I had achieved admiration from other competitors because they understood the work involved in becoming a champion, but when it came to a lifestyle that involved playing the part of a hard man I'd found myself in a world where I didn't belong, a world where I was surrounded by real hard men. I also discovered that even the hardest men on the planet get beaten up by their own minds and find they too are often fighting with themselves. I count myself extremely lucky to have come out of this profession relatively unscathed. I had rung many bells, so to speak, meaning, I can't take back what I've done. My experiences have however made me a stronger, nicer and a more compassionate person though. Some people have not been so fortunate, their split-second decision changing their life forever.

One second they were stopping a fight, the next they are wearing the label KILLER. How do you take someone's life and ever come to terms with it? I'd asked myself this question so many times and I know too many men who are living with this reality. That one, single punch intended to eliminate the 'threat', resulted in them forever known as the guy who killed someone. A murderer. In that scenario, how would you ever not see the faces of all the people affected by your actions? The mother and father of the person you killed, maybe the deceased themselves, wife, children, brothers, sisters, grandparents etc. That punch that took one life but destroyed so many more, now negates everything that comes before the incident and everything after. The label of 'killer' towers above every other aspect of your personality which becomes insignificant, even if for just a brief moment. Even the hardest of men will close their eyes at night and drift into another state of consciousness. They may well be able to control their thoughts and actions whilst awake but their subconscious is waiting to pounce every time the sun goes down.

Chapter #13

The American Nightmare

I reached for the car's heating control, it was -15 degrees Fahrenheit. The windscreen was iced over and I had the driver's window open, my head craned out so I could see the road ahead of me. As I tried to turn on the heating, the knob twisted one way, then the other and then it fell off in my hand. Hardly a surprise given that this vehicle I was driving wasn't exactly what you could call road-worthy! In fact, it turned out to be a camouflage-coloured, pick-up truck, death trap! Not only did it have no heating but the petrol gauge didn't work, the speedometer needle never moved and the power steering was non-existent.

I was living in Carbondale, Illinois, having been recruited to build a karate programme for a local sports centre. It didn't take long for me to realise that the entire set-up by the club manager was pretty much a con-job. Bob was a chancer and liked to skirt around every rule required for running a legitimate business. Unkept promises which had been made to me on the premise of me leaving my life in the UK, a lack of general respect and rules which you wouldn't enforce on your teenage children all became apparent within weeks of arriving and my gut soon told me there was something seriously wrong. But I persevered, determined to turn the set-up into something which could work for me and eventually he'd be off my back and I'd be more independent. Bob was a former champion wrestler, but you would have never guessed this on meeting him, he looked more like he had just walked off the set of the Smurfs. Short in stature with a big belly and snow-white beard but he carried a confidence and arrogance that left everyone in his orbit either in awe of him or in fear of him. In light of his traits I only ever saw someone who might be able to help my cause, so I scratched his back for as long as I needed to.

I'd been introduced to Bob via a friend in Coventry who had been running wrestling sessions with Bob's son, Chris. Chris had travelled from the US to the UK to run some grass-roots wrestling programmes. One afternoon my friend called me and asked me to come over to meet Chris at his house.

Chris and I talked about his dad's set-up in Carbondale and it seemed like the perfect opportunity to get my foot in the door of a country I'd fallen in love with during my early competition days. I just needed to run a karate programme at a local sports club in return for a wage and a visa which would allow me to stay on a semi-permanent basis in the US. It sounded like the perfect opportunity, right?

The meeting went swimmingly, the arrangements seemed flawless. All that was required from me was to enrol at a local college in Carbondale to obtain a student visa so I could stay and work there and Bob, his dad, would take care of all those arrangements. Within a couple of months of meeting Chris this is exactly what happened. Here I was in America, just after Christmas, staying with one of Bob's friends temporarily whilst I got settled and found my feet. Webster (how American?!) was an attorney who lived alone with his two dogs. I'd now become his British 'roomie' and everything seemed to be going to plan. What an awesome adventure!

The Carbondale sports centre was a far cry from what I was used to in the UK. From the main road it looked more like a large, two-storey office building but this was the USA and even hospitals and bars are located in buildings that often look more like a high street shopping mall. As you entered the building there was a small reception on the right, next to what felt like a sea of long, heavy, green curtains. Behind this were half a dozen tennis courts and a door which led to a weights room. My gut told me something was 'off' from the get-go, my very first visit to the sports centre had me questioning everything about the set up I was now a part of, and that was before I'd even met the team around me. As the first few days played out I constantly found myself thinking inwardly, what the fuck have I gotten myself into? 'Ok, this is America, it's a totally different culture so I'm just going to have to get used to how they do things,' was my go-to reasoning. Think, a combination of the movies American Pie and Porky's and you wouldn't be far off from what I was surrounded by.

Low-paid or school-funded college kids on scholarships pretty much ran everything in the sports centre. The weights room was often packed with loud, testosterone-controlled males and cheer leaders (think 'Mean Girls') who were all desperate to not only belong, but also be better than the next person. It didn't take me long to realize that Americans take about ten years longer than their British counter parts to grow the fuck up, puberty in America seems to start at age 10 and last well into their 30's. I'm not slagging Americans off, I'm just stating what I saw/see and it was these very facts that would ultimately drive the nails into the coffin of my first attempt at the American dream. After a long morning at the sports centre, a morning filled with 'what the fuck?' moments, Webster, who later became known as Web, had a surprise for me as we arrived back at the house. We drove up the long, winding driveway leading from the main road onto his property which backed onto a few acres of green land. As we got closer a black and green, camouflage, pickup truck came into view. "This is yours to use while you are here," he said, "You will need to keep your eye on the gas situation as the gas gauge doesn't work, and you won't know what speed you are doing as the speedometer is broken." He's gotta be kidding, right? "Just try and drive behind the slowest car on the road and you'll stay within the speed limits." WTF? "Oh and you'll get a good workout whilst driving as the power steering doesn't work, make sure you keep an eye on the front, left tyre, it goes flat after a few days, and make sure you put oil in every week as it has some sort of leak. We don't want the engine to seize, but apart from that it's a fun little truck!"

He wasn't kidding... about any of this. Only he failed to tell me it would take at least five attempts to start it up each morning and anyone in earshot of the truck whilst the engine was running would think that a fighter jet was about to career through the neighbourhood. It was the kind of truck that whilst driving would attract stares, finger pointing and bewilderment. Today, people would be lining up to take selfies with it. 'This is all part of the adventure,' I told myself.

So here I was in the land of the free where I'd recently just been charged $300 for second-hand college books (WTF?). As the weeks went by I learned that my student visa was only valid if in fact I was a student and that meant I had to actually attend classes, and attend all of them. Not quite what was sold to me during my early conversations with Chris and Bob. I had first enrolled on the Exercise Science course, one which I knew would suit me given my background but there was far too much studying and homework involved, alongside what was becoming a fulltime job at the sports centre. After all, I was only going to college to keep my student visa so I changed my course to something less demanding - Art. I had always been good at art, I absolutely loved sketching so I thought this course would be a great fit for me. How wrong could I have been!

In fact, looking back now the whole college experience was a nightmare, starting with having to pay for books that were literally falling apart at the spine, lining the pockets of the college where they have a system of selling second-hand books at 80% of their original price. When you're done with them they buy back again for 10% of the original price, only to sell them on a third, fourth, fifth, sixth time at, you guessed it, 80% of the original price. In some cases they were just photo copies of the original book, filed into a binder and sold for $50. In isolation it wasn't a huge issue but I was becoming increasingly uncomfortable with the whole set-up in Carbondale, in particular, feeling like I was becoming trapped under Bob's 'regime'.

I'd only been in the States a few months but I'd fast started to recognise that this situation wasn't working for me and I didn't see it getting any better. In fact, the situation was getting worse by the week. Not only wasn't I getting paid the salary that was promised but I was now also being expected to help with many other chores in and around the sports centre. Bob had decided he wanted to take over the running of the bar that was located on the first floor just above the bowling alley. There was a shit load of work needing to be done before the bar was ready to open to the public so everyone was expected to help at the snap of his fingers, for as long as was required and for zero payment. I was more than happy to help out a little and I didn't care about being paid, but this was more than just shifting a few boxes and stacking the bar shelves.

Bob had created this environment where he called the shots and had very skilfully positioned everyone around him in a place of dependency. My accommodation, food and college tuition fees were being funded by the sports centre (Bob) and he wasn't shy in pointing out, that without him, we would all be fucked. Well, I hadn't travelled 4,000 miles to become a prisoner of this little fat smurf and those days of just smiling and sucking up hardship were long behind me. Yes, I was very aware that it would take time to build a karate programme and I was more than willing to accept that my salary was going to ultimately depend on numbers in a class but being told that I had to clean out filthy, grease splattered ovens which took me away from building a club audience was like a red rag to a raging bull.

Everything about this venture felt wrong. I'd spent so many years fighting to find my confidence and in doing so I'd become very intolerant of bullshit and arseholes. But now here I was being bullshitted to by arseholes and it wasn't sitting well with me at all.

I had long adopted the belief that you instruct people how to treat you. My demeanour and personality had told the people that were now in my orbit that I was a nice, respectful and loyal person. Unfortunately it was becoming obvious that Bob and a few others needed to see the bad wolf in action.

Telling my host and financial sponsor that I wasn't happy and things needed to change was never going to go down well though. Bob was the boss, everyone involved in the sports centre all fell in line except for me, and when I questioned him about what my role was and that I thought I was being taken advantage of, things began to get much worse, not better.

Once Bob realised that I wasn't going to be his puppet our relationship changed from pleasant niceties to just tolerating each other. I'd now started to look for my exit strategy and

It wasn't long before I was back on a flight to the UK.

Carbondale had been one hell of an adventure though, not the kind that I'd been expecting of course but It had taught me so much about myself. It was this very trip that showed me how to chase dreams while never expecting to catch them. When I saw everything going to shit, I pretty much just laughed at the situation and imagined myself in the trenches on a bloody, battlefield of war. Sitting in a shit filled hole, surrounded by the enemy wasn't something I was prepared to endure though and just like the famous Roman historian Tacitus said, 'He that fights and runs away, May turn and fight another day; But he that is in battle slain, Will never rise to fight again.' I hadn't failed, I can't fail. I've learned. It was time to retreat, climb out of that hole, gather my thoughts and begin chasing my next dream.

Chapter #14

Dodging a bullet

This book could have quite easily been called "Chasing Dreams" as everything you have read thus far feeds into that narrative. Everyone has dreams, and it's those dreams that get us out of bed each and every day. Having dreams are not the same as chasing them however. Many people will dream of having a big house, a nice car and regular holidays abroad, but those dreams rarely materialize for many, mostly because a lot of people do not have the confidence to either dream big or to actually go after those dreams with real determination. Is this because those dreams are unrealistic given a person's circumstances or could it just be; as I am more inclined to believe; that they fight with themselves in a never-ending battle over self-worth and self-belief?

They have a dream, an idea they would like to follow. They then see obstacles in the way and the fight with themselves begins, " I can't do this, I am not good enough, I will look stupid if I fail etc." The list of 'I can'ts' is an endless one as you find yourself in round after round of stalemate with no clear path to a victory. Some days you win a round, some days you lose one, and some rounds are counted as even, but the rounds have no limit, they keep showing up and you keep fighting, if you get knocked down you get the fuck up. Some days this is harder than others but you never stay down, sure you can take a little break but you should never ever stay down because the most important fight in life isn't with anyone else; your most important fight is always going to be with yourself.

I wanted to be confident and be a someone. It was only me who knew what that meant. I wanted to be a good competitive fighter so I looked at what was required to make that happen. I saw a guy wearing an England badge on his karate gi jacket. This badge represented an international standard competitor and I wanted one of those badges. I wanted one so badly that it became an obsession; it was always going to happen.

I ordered it. I ate, slept, dreamed and talked about it, like it was already mine. The dream walked side by side with reality. The dream then gave way and reality took over. As an athlete I had competed in the USA. I then had that same crazy burning desire. I not only wanted to live in the States, I wanted to become an American citizen so I went ahead and ordered that too.

I was now living in Indianapolis, Indiana and I had gained a fascination with the fitness and weight-loss industry, mainly because the ability to lose weight and get fitter required a similar personality switch that I'd worked on my entire life, applying the same logic of creating 'someone (an alter ego) ' to do the job for me. I had personally become ready to start my own weight-loss and fitness journey as I myself had gained a considerable amount of weight and I'd lost a lot of the fitness that I had worked so hard for. Of course I already had the knowledge, I understood how to workout, I knew what I needed to do, the only thing that was lacking was the motivation, something that I'd never struggled with in the past. As a competitive athlete my motivation came from having to be ready for the next competition. As a karate instructor my motivation came from my students, but now I had to find that motivation from somewhere else.

I had always enjoyed a tough workout and a good sweat but it had been competitive karate that was that driving force. I had also gotten into weight training but the bulking diet that I had adopted had been done all wrong and the bulk that I had gained was pretty much all fat. It was then that a friend back in the UK contacted me asking if I would be interested in meeting up with him in Las Vegas; he had been invited to teach a self-protection session at the Chuck Norris convention. Of course I jumped at the opportunity and just a few weeks later I was waking up in sin city.

At this convention I was given the opportunity to run a sport (competitive) karate session for the Chuck Norris competition teams. Wow, the skinny shy kid from Coventry who had run away from confrontations was teaching fighting techniques to a group headed by the man who fought Bruce Lee in the movie, 'Way of The Dragon'; this surely must be a dream.

After my session was over I sat and watched a guy who was running a group fitness workout. Garrett was a Hollywood stuntman who was a close friend of Mr Norris and had worked on many of the Texas Rangers episodes. He was also a former student of Billy Blanks, the guy behind the TaeBo craze at the time, and it was Garrett's session that not only captured my attention but also my imagination; there it was, I had my motivation, my next dream to chase. I wanted to be able to run workouts like that.

That evening saw an awards ceremony with Chuck Norris giving out trophies and medals to the winners of the competition that had been held the previous day. He was also presenting awards to actors and crew from the Texas Rangers show. Garrett handed me a video camera and asked if I could record him receiving his stuntman award. We then sat and chatted over a few beers. I told him that I was very interested in the workout that he had taught and he promptly invited me to his home in California.

With this trip now on my calendar it was time for me to get back to some serious training. I'd forgotten just how important motivation actually was but now I had a goal to shoot for. Not only was I working on my own fitness but also on becoming properly certified in running classes I studied for and gained my group fitness, personal training and lifestyle & weight management certifications as I prepared to become a full time group fitness coach, and a short time later here I was landing in Los Angeles.

When I got to Garrett's gym and actually watched his own classes in action I was blown away. The classes were what I would describe as adults' karate without any martial intent, meaning: no one in the class was talking about or focused on real combat. This was a fitness class and although their kicks and punches would put many traditional karate clubs to shame, their focus was on fitness, agility and producing aesthetic physiques. Well this was Hollywood and everyone in this class wanted to be perfect, and they were. Watching non-karate adults producing such excellent techniques was awe inspiring, but what was even more mind blowing was the fact that if these adults had been asked to wear karate uniforms and go through karate gradings (belt testing) then everyone of them would quit. I was witnessing karate repackage as a form of exercise. It was brilliant and by the looks of the physiques it was producing you could see why the class was full of Hollywood's elite.

Garrett was married (estranged) from his then wife, who was previously married to the actor, Joe Pesci, and Garrett's close friend was the " The Great One" Wayne Gretzky. This was nuts, a Willenhall kid, with no academic qualifications who had struggled with confidence most of his life was now surrounded by movie stars, sports personalities and multimillionaires. Wait, no, it's not nuts at all. This is what happens when you get off your ass and believe in yourself, I had more than earned my place at this table. I was not only mixing with celebrities I was also working with them. One other name that I am sure anyone, " of my generation at least" will know of, was Catherine Bach (Daisy Duke) from the Dukes of Hazzard. Catherine was preparing for her return as Daisy Duke in the new Dukes of Hazzard movie that was then in production and she'd asked me to help her with some fight moves for a scene. Yep, I was definitely in Hollywood.

Ok, time to get down to business. Fourteen days of two gruelling group fitness sessions per day, immersing myself in the subject matter and I felt myself becoming the person I needed to become in order to realise my next dream. Wow, in such a very small space of time I'd already begun walking side by side with yet another reality, but I needed to keep this reality alive and present. I knew exactly what I needed to do. When those two weeks came to an end, I said my farewells to Garrett, then I headed back to Indianapolis and within a week I had begun looking for a place to get my own classes started.

I walked into a gym and approached the guy at reception and asked him if they were looking for group fitness instructors. I had now become very good at asking for something without being worried about a negative response, "I don't fail, I only learn." Well, a negative response was exactly what I got, " Not at the moment, we have all our classes pretty much covered," was the reply. Undeterred I followed up with, " OK, can I leave my number and if you find yourself short of an instructor please let me know?"

"Well actually, hum, we may need someone who can run a cardio kickboxing style class in a few weeks to cover for someone who is going on vacation." " I'm your man." I didn't care how much they were paying, I just needed to get my foot in the door and work my way up. " Remember, if you are given an opportunity, say yes then figure out how to do it later."

My very first group fitness class was going to be at the workout Centre in Carmel Indiana, and was indeed due to an instructor going on vacation and I was going to be just covering her classes. I had been given a few weeks' notice about when I would be needed so I spent as much time as possible practising, getting used to moving to a beat and counting down to transitioning from one move to the next. It looked so bloody easy watching the pros do it but what the fuck have I got myself into?

To understand the sort of class I would be running, I went along the week prior to see how the regular instructor worked the room. I opened the main door to the gym and immediately heard the thumping beat of the class already in session. As I approached the workout room the music became louder and I could hear the instructor's commands through the speakers, and now the class is cheering. I walked up to the workout room entrance and popped my head in. Oh shit it was a wall to wall sweat fest and just like I had witnessed in California, everyone in there was motivated by their desire to look perfect, but it was this quest for perfection that had lured me into this profession. As a competitive athlete I had set myself a very high bar, and as someone involved in combat training that was meant to work in a street fight, I had to know I could actually make it work. And now that I was embarking on this new career I wasn't about to lower that bar, so the goal was to stay in touch with Garrett and learn from one of the best in the business but then this happened.

"Hollywood stuntman shot on doorstep mafia style." "Joe Pesci's ex-wife Claudia Marty Haro has been arrested for attempted murder after a hitman failed to kill her husband." Garrett had been gunned down, shot four times when he opened his door at his home in Agoura Hills, California.

Garrett survived but lost his left eye. Claudia was ultimately found guilty of hiring a hitman and sentenced to 12 years for attempted murder. It hadn't really occurred to me at the time but after reading the police reports about how the hitman had scoped out his target, it became clear that just maybe I myself had dodged a bullet, given that I had spent two weeks at Garrett's home often answering the door, and I would have been there while this hit was being planned. Garrett went on to continue in the movie industry and is a very successful stunt coordinator. We still chat from time to time and I would like to thank him for his permission in using his story in this chapter. God bless you my friend.

⊷⊶⊱⟨⟩⊰⊷⊶

Chapter #15

Happy Fat

A perfect example of the ability or inability to recognise how perception plays a role in a person's actions/inactions is the conversation surrounding weight loss, or should I say weight and size management? The weight loss industry was estimated at over $3bn for the year 2022/2023, although some sources suggest it's far greater than that. But why is weight loss a subject that is so easy to understand yet so difficult to achieve? This is literally the billion-dollar question.

We now live in a time where any information is available 24 hours a day, 7 days a week and you can literally find out everything you need to know about how to lose weight with just a simple click of the mouse. So, if we agree that it's not the lack of information that is the problem, then we need to look elsewhere to find out what's going on. Here is a question I ask all my weight loss clients. "If you were locked in a room for many months and you were provided with weighed and measured portions of food, with just enough nourishment to keep you in a daily calorie deficit, do you agree that you would lose weight?" Every single person responded, "Yes, a daily calorie deficit would do the trick." I'd then ask them to go and do their own research. You, the reader, can do the same research yourself right now. Open your search engine and type these words: 'Does a calorie deficit make you lose weight?' There's no magic formula or something special that people who lose weight have discovered. It's basic, simple nature. You already know exactly how it works because often it was a calorie surplus that made you gain weight, right? Now, in your search engine type these words, 'calorie surplus'. I know I have over simplified things here but that's because it really is that simple.

So, now back to my original statement, "How is something so easy to understand so difficult to do?" The answer is also very simple, "You can't do it, and you never will be able to. The reason the weight loss industry is so profitable is because their customers are returning customers, in fact most are customers for life.

My own personal, internal battles had resulted in me approaching difficult situations as another person, a separate alter-ego and this was what I was now teaching my clients how to do. I did this by having them be totally honest with themselves about why they wanted to lose weight in the first place. I'd often tell them, "I've never met anyone who decided to initially lose weight based solely on the number they saw on the scale. Sure, that number became a factor but only after other factors had presented themselves first."

When their own honesty was revealed, I would hear comments such as, "My clothes are too tight, I have no energy, I'm ashamed of the way I look," etc. When probed a little further, these comments are often followed by, "I have a very low self-esteem, no confidence in myself, I feel scared of the world."

Explaining to someone at my weight-loss class that they themselves are the problem, doesn't go down very well at first, as you can imagine. But given that most of these people say they've tried everything and nothing's worked, they are often willing to at least listen to any ideas. "There are many things you will never be able to accomplish as 'you', because 'you' are your lifestyle, your social circle, your family, your job etc and you will never stick to anything that your lifestyle doesn't support."

"We really don't need to try and reinvent the wheel here, if you give nature what she needs, she will give you what you want. The concept of a calorie deficit is as true today as it has been since the beginning of time. It's not whether it works or not, it's whether you can stay with it."

Anyone who approaches weight-loss 'as themselves' are guaranteed to hit a roadblock, but the truth is people looking to lose weight are not looking to lose weight at all, they're looking to lose body fat. There, I said it! The three-letter word that sends most overweight people into an uncontrollable rage and turns even the most polite and reasonable into a devil. In my experience the word 'fat' is such a hot-button issue that most in the weight-loss industry steer away from using it. It isn't good for business, so they replace the word fat with the word 'weight' even though the weight you are looking to lose is mainly body fat. So, let's just call it 'body transformation'.

So, what does body transformation even mean? Everyone who walks out of the barbers or hairdressers knows how different they feel, especially if they haven't had a trim in a while. Something as simple as making their hair shorter or changing their hairstyle can have a crazy-positive impact on a person's confidence and for someone who's drastically gone from very long to very short, it can totally transform their appearance. When it comes to weight-loss it's often a different appearance that many people are going for. As a personal trainer I rarely hear clients say they need to drop weight only to be healthier, although this is often part of their overall goal. What most people are going for is to look and feel better about themselves. They don't take before and after photos showing better blood pressure or clogged/unclogged arteries, it's always a picture of them with their fitter, slimmer looking body.

There are millions of weight loss clubs around the world that are full of people who have been attending for many years and they're still trying to shift the same weight they first arrived with. They lost some weight, gained a few class awards, then lost interest and quit altogether. Having then regained the weight they originally lost (and more) they returned to the same slimming club that they stopped attending last time. Unfortunately, most people never reach their goal, or if they do they don't manage to maintain that achievement. I don't claim to be a body transformation expert, but I do claim to be someone who transformed his body and I've helped many others to do the same.

This is the first book I have written. I'm not a writer per se, or at least not an accomplished writer yet, but as I'm writing this chapter I am once again reminded what a massive task it is that I have undertaken. Writing a little each day then ignoring it for a week or two when I don't feel like writing means I'd be finishing the book in a matter of years rather than months. Unless I become an author, immerse myself and dedicate the time and effort required I will lose interest and quit altogether. I write and I talk about each chapter every day. I look at what I have written just before I go to bed so I can dream about it. I imagine what the cover will look like and how the book will be promoted. People who are around me every day know about the chapter I am writing, I talk about it as my way of keeping it alive. In fact, during my sparring session this morning, I made a point of talking about how fighters lose weight to compete. Competitive fighters are not necessarily weight-loss experts or dietitians. Yes at the very top of their professional ranks these experts are hired but even amateur boxers, competitive bodybuilders and figure athletes have all figured out how to shed weight with a target date in mind and the one underlying attribute they all possess is becoming the person they need to be in order to produce the person they wanted to see.

Change your perception, change your reality. This is how you achieve absolutely everything. What do you see when you visualise all that weight gone? What do you see as your daily life from now on? Weight loss is a massive full time commitment and you are either all the way in or all the way out, there are no halfway measures, but what does all the way in actually look like?

Mike and Kim both showed up at one of my workout classes after a friend told them about how successful class members had been in dropping the pounds. They were both very overweight, Mike more so than Kim but both morbidly obese. We spoke honestly very early in their weight-loss journey about lifestyle and how doing this together as a couple could be a double-edged sword for them. "You can be a great support system for each other, but if one falls off the wagon then it's not uncommon for the other to follow," I explained. They were both excited to get started and I introduced them to a like-minded group who had all made brilliant progress on their transformation. It wasn't long before they'd exchanged contact details of others in the group and their journey had begun. About three months had passed and I'd only seen Mike a handful of times but Kim had become a three-sessions-per-week lady. She hadn't yet noticeably dropped enough weight but her whole demeanour had changed. She'd signed up for a personal training session to start working out in the weights room as she felt it was time for her to work on building a little more muscle, something that she had initially said she would never be interested in.

A personal trainer is far more than someone who just helps you with a workout. They're often someone a client opens up to and shares a little dirty laundry with now and then and this is exactly what Kim did. Kim was committed, she'd found a new purpose, new friends in the class and in turn a new confidence. She had indeed awoken an alter ego but her husband didn't get along with the 'new' Kim at all. In fact, Kim's alter ego and Mike were fighting all the time and Kim was losing her shit just trying to keep the peace. Mike was no longer on board, she told me. He was her husband, her soul mate, the love of her life, they had teenage boys who they both lived for but Mike was now making things difficult and so were the boys. "How do I get them to see that this is very important to me?" Kim asked. But I didn't have an answer. "Mike wants the 'old' me back, the one who drinks a few beers in front of the firepit and shares a big, crusty pizza with the family." When I explained that indulging very occasionally won't hurt, "but Mike doesn't do 'occasionally'!" was her reply.

As the months went by Kim's determination went from strength to strength, she continued working out and dropping weight consistently. She was 100lb down and now unrecognizable from the person who had first shown up. Our chats continued and she shared with me how Mike now resented what he referred to as her 'obsession' with this new life and that she, in turn, resented his lack of support. He'd accused her of wanting to be attractive to other men and couldn't understand why she couldn't just be happy the way she was before.

When someone decides they are going to lose weight they do so without understanding what they are really signing up for and what is required. This is understandable given the complex journey which lies ahead. Kim had employed the help of her alter ego. I'd taught her how to summon it, listen to it and she was a very willing student. Kim had found a new confidence that had her dressing and behaving differently, the new Kim was now mixing with people who were into fitness challenges for charity which led her to enroll for a half marathon. This meant regular training meets at a running club where she met more new friends, who in turn invited her to new social events which presented her with even more new friends. The knock-on effect associated with weight loss can't be overstated and is exactly why most people discontinue their journey and why ultimately, Kim unfortunately stopped. Yes, she'd been successful, she'd learned how to diet and had adopted a regular exercise regime, one that would have taken her to a weight and 'look' that she thought she wanted, but like so many other people Kim discovered that she didn't like the new version of herself very much. She'd changed so much physically but hadn't adapted to the change emotionally, she felt like she was always fighting with this alter ego who was overbearing and so demanding. "Life was a lot easier when I was fat!" she'd say. Crikey, if I had a penny for every time I've heard that during my career! My response to her was the same as every other time I'd heard that said, "Being in shape isn't something you do, it's someone you are and most people can't become that person."

Kim came less and less to class and eventually stopped coming altogether. She went back to her old life, gained all the weight back plus more and to my knowledge had accepted that she will always be overweight because she doesn't want to live the lifestyle necessary to not be. I know a lot of people who have been regular gym rats and fitness classes junkies for many years but haven't lost any weight or changed their body shape at all and this is because they show up at the gym or their class as them, a person who is showing up for an hour, coasting through the class physically, but not feeling the class emotionally. They show up because they love the people there, they feel connected to the atmosphere that this generates, they truly believe that this group has changed their life. And they're right, the group may well have changed their life but has it really changed them?

Think about this, could you jump into the cockpit of an airplane without the required training? Of course not. However, millions of people throw themselves into weight loss before understanding how it all works. They jump in hoping that something will feel different this time, that it will be easier than the last time, when in reality the first three months of any weight loss endeavour is just the tuition phase. Even if a good amount of weight is lost during this time, you are still fact finding and understanding how to overcome the various obstacles in the way of your quest to find a better body. Three months is just the learning stage, but for most people it will be 90 days of hell that they will want to be over in a flash. Yes, it takes a good few months of self-awareness training before you arrive at the place where the real body transformation can start, but most people will jump feet first into that cockpit and are frustrated when they can't take off straight away.

Now, these days when anyone asks me for weight loss advice it is always this - three months to sort out your head, nine months to be reborn. If you can't commit to twelve months then you're preparing to fail. Losing weight is and always will be a very difficult subject to address, the process is very simple to understand though. The energy (calories) you put in, needs to be less than energy out but this is over simplifying things. Someone who doesn't 100% believe in the process will quit when it doesn't quite go the way they'd planned. Many people will never be comfortable living the lifestyle that is required to lose and then maintain that loss, and it's the word 'lifestyle' that is pretty much the key to everything; combined with your perception of that lifestyle is how major changes are made.

Chapter #16
Hard Target

I'd asked everyone in the class to find a partner and introduce themselves. We'd just finished a group fitness workout and always ended the session with some focus-mitt drills, mostly for fun, but also to build some understanding of the techniques used in the group workout. My classes mainly consisted of women but there were a handful of steadfast, die-hard men who loved the workout too. Some were husbands/partners of the women in the group, but there was also something about the workout that attracted both sexes even though the entire class required movement to a music beat, something that many men wouldn't feel comfortable with.

"Maybe we could do a self-defence class sometime?" one of the ladies asked. It got me wondering about the nature of the class and their appetite to learn something slightly more advanced. Wondering what had triggered the question, I asked if there was a particular reason why self-defence interested her. She said that knowing my background maybe it would be a good opportunity to learn what really worked opposed to some of the stuff she had seen before. "Real self-defence/ self-protection is basically brutal, very violent and not for the faint of heart," I responded. The class became intrigued and pushed the issue. They at least wanted to hear my opinion. I agreed and enquired as to whether any of the class had been attacked for no apparent reason; the kind of situation where you'd been standing minding your own business, no words were spoken and no altercation had taken place. Silence filled the room for a moment while the class paused to reflect, then one by one they shook their heads. "No, never," a few of the group muttered. This was exactly the answer I expected as it's the same answer I get whenever this question is asked. Occasionally someone will say that they have been mugged but even then the mugger had often set them up with some dialogue.

"So, if you have never been attacked, why do you want to learn self-defence?" Again, a few moments of silence, then one guy answered, "In case we get into a fight with someone I guess." "You shouldn't be getting into a fight," I answered. "If you have the option not to fight, why would you choose to fight?" The class fell deathly silent again as they searched for a feasible reply, so I posed another question. "Now what do you think constitutes an attack and what do you believe you need to learn to be able to protect yourself from it?" "Well, it could be anything I guess," came the reply. "So how do you protect yourself from an endless list of scenarios?" "I guess we just need a gun," was one answer.

I ran a small gym in Indianapolis which catered for group fitness, personal training and boxing clientele. I rarely spoke about my other life in the UK where I'd spent close to fifteen years dealing with the brutal violence that went hand in hand with door work. I continued, "This is exactly why I don't teach self-defence classes, and if I decided to, it would focus on offence not defence." Now the class really wanted to know more but the chap who had declared, 'maybe we just need a gun', said, "Well, that's why we have the second amendment in America."

Being a Brit who had not grown up in an environment where carrying a gun for protection was an accepted reality, I offered a completely different spin on the subject, which of course sparked the debate even further. "So, who in here carries a gun?" I enquired. The room collectively shook their heads, none of them carried a gun. "OK, now who owns a gun?" I remember about eight of them saying they owned a gun which was safely locked away at home. This blew my mind. "So, you have a gun which is locked away in one room in your house, but to access it you need to get the key, unlock the safe, remove the gun…. Under what circumstances?" I asked. There was complete silence, until one lady replied, "I'd need to load the gun first as I don't like having a loaded gun in the house, we have small children." I probed further as I wanted to understand how owning a gun made them feel safer and after a bit of back and forth, the only conclusion that I could reach was that it was better to have and not need, than to need and not have. Having a gun in the house brought peace of mind, especially at night.

The group of people in front of me were not street-wise or living a life surrounded by violence but they lived in a country which permitted the shooting of someone who was breaking into their home. Most of them had never even fired a gun let alone pointed one at an intruder, so the odds of them being able to control the fear during a home invasion were very questionable. It certainly wasn't my intention to get into a debate over guns. Americans love their firearms and perhaps this was a conversation best left to the politicians, but the 'owning of a weapon for the purpose of self-defence' conversation was now very much out there and I became increasingly fascinated. The more we talked the more it became clear that owning a gun was sort of like a country owning nuclear weapons. "Nobody invades a country that has nukes," one guy eloquently pronounced, adding, "a gun in the house is a great deterrent, right?" He did of course have a valid point, just the assumption that every home in the United States was armed would, to some degree at least, make some people, opportunists think twice. The career criminal, home invaders, however have most likely done their homework and not only are they armed themselves but they actually know how to use those weapons. It was this very point that I was now trying to get across. The subject of weapons quickly moved on and the guy who had said 'in case we get into a fight,' wanted to understand what I meant when I said that "you shouldn't be getting into fights".

I then dropped this bombshell comment that stunned the room.

"Men rarely ever get physically attacked."

Err, what? Men rarely ever get physically attacked, how is that statement true? Of course this sounded ludicrous and needed a proper explanation. "Men don't get attacked, it's most often their ego that takes the hit. It's then their inability to control that ego that results in them being involved in a fight. I asked the question earlier, 'when have you ever been attacked for absolutely no reason?' You all responded 'never,' yes even the men." I then explained to everyone why I didn't really get involved in self-defence classes anymore. "The syllabus for 'real' self-defence is so small that it doesn't warrant regular training sessions, once you know what to do, you just have to keep drilling it yourself." Yes, I teach people what to do, but then they're on their own. I don't teach people to fight, other than competitively. Although I do teach people how to become a hard target because that is the key to real self-protection.

My philosophy is to take 100% control of all confrontations, leaving my destiny in my hands and not a stranger's. I view all potential altercations the same way. The vast majority of volatile situations can be walked away from, but in the absence of this option and with absolutely no chance of escape, my goal is to strike first and put the threat to sleep using a knock-out. For example, a rapist puts a knife to their victim's throat and states that they will not be hurt if they do as they are told. Choosing to believe that the perpetrator will keep their word is all the victim has to keep them safe in that situation. The only reason you would believe that a mugger will leave you alone if you hand over what they demand, is because to believe any other outcome is far too terrifying to comprehend.

Personally, leaving the outcome of my fate in the aggressor's hands is inconceivable and I've lost count of how many times I've had to use a knock-out punch to end something before it had even started. I know that even if I had a knife to my throat I would at least be searching for that window of opportunity to strike. I don't believe that giving somebody money in a mugging situation is necessarily always going to make the mugger just go away. Of course, every situation is different but once you decide to give up control then your fate is totally in their hands.

I'd watched a short video clip on YouTube taken from a CCTV camera inside a hospital. A young nurse was standing in a corridor when a large, drunken man grabbed her and started to slap her. She stood directly in front of him while he shouted into her face, and he proceeded to grab and push her over. She eventually stood up, only to be knocked to the floor again and kicked whilst on the ground. Of course, the camera didn't capture how terrifying this experience was for this poor, young lady, nor does it accurately capture the strength and aggression of the attacker. I did note however that it captured the window of opportunity this lady had to deliver a knock-out punch and regain control, but she was of course unaware that she had this potential so it never occurred to her.

Fifteen years as a bouncer taught me that defending yourself means staying a few steps ahead in any situation, and that means understanding and coping with the disabling effects of fear. I only needed to be proficient in a few very basic techniques, techniques that pretty much anyone could learn in just a few hours but I've learnt that not everyone will be able to apply those techniques. Imagine winning an F16 fighter jet, a machine which was created for military purposes with missiles capable of flattening a city. If the average Joe was given that jet and had it parked outside their home all they would really have was a multi-million dollar heap of metal that was useless to them. But in the possession of a highly qualified fighter pilot, it could be used with devastating effect.

My point here is we all own a fighter jet, (knockout punch) metaphorically speaking, but most people never get in the cockpit and so never figure out the controls. It took me many years of mental training to be able to deliver just a few brutal seconds of awesomeness. I told this class that I'd become very passionate about sharing what I had discovered, showing others that they also could tap into another version of themselves to accomplish difficult tasks, while at the same time recognising that most people would never really entertain the notion that it was even possible when it came to having to be violent.

"So how do you teach people to become a hard target?" I guess I should have expected that one. The answer, although simple, doesn't happen overnight. It's a process that happens over time but mostly involves reprogramming your current victim mentality. Put simply, dogs don't get attacked because they will bite your fucking bollocks off. Dogs are hard targets because they only have one technique that they use every single time.

Chapter #17

Two Million Copies Sold

While researching a topic online a little while ago I came across a book that was of interest to me. I'd never heard of this book before, never seen it advertised anywhere and had never heard anyone even talking about it. I mention all of this because I ordered this book and when it arrived I was absolutely amazed at what I saw printed on the front cover.

'1.5 million copies sold.' How can this be so? How can a book that nobody seems to know about be so crazy-successful? Maybe this was just a marketing ploy, perhaps the author put that figure on the cover to make people believe that this was a hugely successful book, thus gathering more interest. Maybe they were just lying though and if they were, did that even matter?

As someone who was currently writing a book myself I understandably wanted to find out more about the 1.5 million copies sold so I dug a little deeper. I discovered that there was no ploy, no lie, this book was indeed a best-seller. It was first printed back in the early 90's and had quite a few reprints, second and third editions etc. So, no, this book wasn't an overnight success, it had taken over 30 years to reach these sales figures. But wait, a million and a half sales in 30 years is amazing, right? What was even more amazing though was the fact that for at least the first ten years after publication, there was no such thing as the internet, so the millions, no, billions of people that can now be reached via social media across the entire planet nowadays, wasn't even a thing back then. My mind was now working overtime. If this book, a mediocre book at that, could generate those kinds of figures and during a time where it was predominantly only sold in bookstores, then what could my own book be capable of?

'Two Million copies sold' appeared as a huge wall, an obstacle in front of me. This was my next venture, my new goal, but is that even realistic? Just hearing myself ask that question awakened a bunch of emotions (alter egos) which collectively lifted me up and screamed, 'If you believe you can, you can; if you believe you can't then you're right!' I began looking to my past, reflecting on all the hurdles I'd either climbed over or in many cases, smashed down. I heard the voice of a renowned TV psychologist, 'the best predictor of future behaviour is past behaviour.' He was right, I'd always begun a new adventure feeling vulnerable and unworthy of achieving the goals I'd visualised, while at the same time totally prepared to give it my best shot.

Turning back life's pages and looking at the previous chapters is something we all do and something we should do because those chapters shaped our lives. While writing this book I have been forced to revisit the past and as I do so I'm reminded that regrets and what if's have no place in my psyche. I can't change anything from the past so giving those thoughts a place to live in my head is just cluttering up space that could be better utilised. With that said, I do regularly reflect on times gone by as a way of reminding myself of where I came from. Notice, I said 'reflect', not 'dwell'. The past can't be changed but it's past experiences that really matter to me.

As a child and a young adult my own personality wasn't brave or tough but the only person who knew this about me was me. When I had looked at Jay and Gobshite, my perception of them was that they were tough confident lads who could have a fight, but I was wrong and when I looked at myself, my perception was that I was weak and scared but I was wrong about that too. If reality was based on perception, all I had to do was change my perception and my reality would change also. It all sounded pretty simple but it would take a lot of work to understand how this was going to play out. The only reason I'm able to write this book is because my perception of the end product is that it'll be a bestseller, that millions of people are going to want to read this book. If my perception was that I may be able to, if I am lucky, sell a few copies to a few close friends then I wouldn't have the drive or the patience to complete this venture. When I started training at my first karate club, I showed up there as a beginner with zero knowledge but within a few weeks I had handed over the reins to my actor ego who perceived himself as a champion waiting to be recognised.

Of course, at the time I didn't know I was doing this, I just did it. It was as though I was walking with a guardian angel who took control when I felt lost, scared and vulnerable. I watched what the instructors were doing, copied them and immersed myself in the role of a karate champion. I acted like one, so I looked like one, and other students around me had the perception that I was one. In a class of over thirty people I stood out, not because I was capable necessarily, but because everyone believed I was capable. My actor ego made me feel like a someone and then over time reality caught up.

In the second chapter of this book, 'Scared', I'm every young child who was fighting with the unknown more than anything else. How scary was your first visit to the dentist, first time on a plane or moving up to senior school? In the absence of facts we fill in the blanks with a perception, maybe this perception was a result of something someone told you like when my Mum told me that the Vords lived on the river bank disguised as pancakes. I'd never seen them but in my nightmares they were very real. Just like I had never seen Jay or Gobshite have a fight but everyone was scared of them, so I just thought I should be also.

I know for certain that some of you reading this have thought very seriously about turning your skills into a full-time business, however you may have a perception that you will fail and be seen as a failure by those around you. If this is the case, you need to become fail-proof by dialling down what you perceive as successful. I've stated that I'm going to sell millions of copies of this book. This statement for me is simply an affirmation of intent. If I sell very few books I have still been successful because I've written and published a book with the intention of selling millions of copies. As a group fitness instructor my intention was to run fitness classes for groups. As a personal trainer my intention was to take on individuals and small groups for personal training sessions. I achieved both, I never attached a number of people required in a class or a monetary amount I needed to validate myself as having been successful. If I'd told myself 'I need to sell millions of copies of my book otherwise I am a failure,' then I'm setting myself up for disaster with an unrealistic goal but that doesn't mean it's not going to happen.

I know countless karate instructors who are stuck in the same chapter, so to speak. They have boat loads of experience and a ton of skills to offer outside of karate but they only see themselves as karate instructors so they continue running poorly-attended classes in often less than adequate facilities. Turning the page and beginning a new chapter can be very difficult, especially when your perception of who you are and what you do has been ingrained for many years. Once I realised that everything was based on my own personal perception I was able to create my own realities, ones that worked for me and my lifestyle and not just blindly follow what was considered normal. A thousand people can all be looking out of the same window and all see the same landscape but their perception of what they see will be different depending on their viewpoint. A businessman may see financial opportunities, a homeless person may be looking for a safe place to sleep, a criminal may see people he can prey on and an animal lover may well see a place to sit and watch the wildlife. When I realised that everyone sees the world through their own individual, unique lens, I embraced my own lens and took care of building my own future, whilst working hard not to judge others not knowing what they see through their window. I only know what I see; I see a world full of possibilities where new chapters are waiting to be written.

As a young child I perceived myself as weak, someone destined to be one of life's spectators. I regularly told myself that real men were brave, they were protectors. I could have never seen myself as being able to protect myself let alone anyone else, but once my perception changed so did that reality. Understanding that everyone sees the world through their own reality was and is actually quite comforting, it taught me not to judge people based on my own perceptions.

As a young karate instructor with my own clubs I had someone whom I saw as a business partner. We ran the clubs together and it never once occurred to me over the years that he may have seen things differently to me. I showed up at the club one evening and he wasn't there. Assuming that he couldn't make it for some reason, I called his house the next day but there was no answer, I was a little concerned. The following evening I showed up at the club and once again he wasn't there. I also noticed that a few of the regulars were missing. I later learned that nothing had happened to him, but he'd started his own clubs and had taken a few of our class members with him. Even back then in my early twenties I somehow managed to chalk this up as one of life's experiences. At first, I was angry which quickly turned into disappointment. No, I wasn't angry with him, I was just disappointed in him. In my world we'd been running clubs together, both pulling in the same direction. His perception was quite different. My perception at the time was that we were of equal ability, while he was under the impression I thought of myself as the kingpin and he wasn't happy playing second fiddle. I took a hard look at myself and wondered if maybe I'd pushed him away making him feel like that, but then I heard from a good few people that he'd been building his own clubs for a while, having always just wanted to do his own thing. He understandably wanted to be the kingpin in his own domain. It was many years later that I read a book called the 48 Laws of Power by Robert Greene. The first three laws explain perfectly what I'd experienced.

Law # 1 Never Outshine the Master

Always make those above you feel comfortably superior. In your desire to please or impress them, do not go too far in displaying your talents or you might accomplish the opposite – inspire fear or insecurity.

Law #2. Never Put Too Much Trust in Friends

Learn How to Use Enemies. Friends are more likely to betray you in haste as they are more prone to envy. However, if you hire a former enemy, they will prove themselves more trustworthy, as they have more to prove.

Law #3 Conceal Your Intentions

Hide your intentions not by closing up (with the risk of appearing secretive and making people suspicious) but by talking endlessly about your desires and goals— just not your real ones.

I was now older and wiser. I chose and still choose not to verbalise everything I see and think, instead I just let fate play out. The chips will land where they land, as the saying goes.

A friend, a very good friend, had received a phone call from a businessman who was interested in partnering with him and taking his venture to the next level. My friend met the businessman and agreed on the partnership even though he hadn't yet told me anything about it. I'd been given the heads-up by a mutual acquaintance though, so when my friend called me to explain I acted clueless. To be fair, what he'd been offered was a much better and lucrative deal than we had together. But what still played on my mind was that I'd bent over backwards to help and support my friend, making sure I included him in every opportunity that came my way. He on the other hand seemed only interested in feathering his own nest.

I'm sure neither of the guys I've mentioned see it the way I did. I was shit on though, but this is real life, it happens. My humble ego laughed about it, brushed himself down and wished them both the best of luck. I hold no ill will or animosity towards either of them, they did what was best for them at the time.

Chapter #18

Live it, Become it.

'Live it, become it.' I coined this phrase one day while talking to a group about weight loss, "If you live the life of a thin person, you will become thin." It's a simple concept to grasp and one that became the answer to every goal I wanted to achieve, and in fact, the answer to everything I didn't want. The law of attraction is very real yet very misunderstood. I'd experienced first-hand how the power of manifestation through desire really worked but I'd also discovered that many people were confused about the process. Of course, I can only share my own experience and how it's worked for me. I can't however promise that it'll work the same for you. In a nutshell, those who practise aspirational thinking will understand that what you have in your life now, is the result of past thoughts and actions. Like most people, I'd been ordering my own fate through the choices and decisions I'd made, oblivious of their impact on my life. Once I realised this I was able to order my future with a better understanding of what to expect.

So let me explain how it works for me so you can at least get a little understanding of your own possible potential. First, I think it would be best to explain how I know it doesn't work. Many people who are struggling financially and have seen information about manifesting wealth by asking the universe for help, may well have just assumed that all they had to do was to think, wish or even pray that money would come their way. Perhaps even asking for a big lottery win. This is probably the textbook example of what doesn't happen. The universe doesn't take your order and just deliver it to you while you sleep, you must be actively involved and make continued amendments, contributions to that order. Did you have an idea today? Where did that idea suddenly come from? If it wasn't in your head yesterday, why is it there now? Your thoughts ultimately create your reality. The universe hears those thoughts and provides you with opportunities and choices which allow you to build on that thought. It plants the seed and guides you to the bottom rung of the ladder.

This book is the perfect example of how that works. I wanted something that was mine, something that had the potential to generate an income without me having to show up in person to conduct personal training sessions. My thoughts had focused on being able to sell something globally without being physically restricted to any location. Working as a personal trainer and group fitness instructor required me to commit to a specific location and I wanted to break free from that commitment. 'Write a book!' was the obvious direction. for me. But for me, that once quiet kid who'd struggled with self-confidence from such a young age, writing a book had never felt in the realms of possibilities. 'I'm not a writer though, I wouldn't even know where to start,' I kept telling myself. I put the idea away and worked on looking for something else, but as I did, I kept seeing signs, encouraging me to revisit my decision. The final one was - 'Don't start a business, write a book' - the heading of an article I stumbled across on my Facebook feed. But this is how it all works. When you want something, you think about it, subsequently those thoughts create a sequence of prompts that you either act on or ignore.

Here's another great example. A young man watches a movie about big-rig truckers who drive across the USA in huge 18-wheeler vehicles. He becomes inspired and dreams of doing that job. This young man lives in a little town in Belgium though, thousands of miles away from America and at the time of watching the movie he doesn't even possess a basic driving licence. If he asked the universe to make him a US trucker he wouldn't wake up the next morning and find himself cruising along Route 66, of course! He may simply bump into a friend who was on his way for some driving lessons, which in turn may result in signing up for lessons himself, thus beginning his journey to his dream. Each decision point in his life is his to own and ultimately shape his future.

Back to the online article, I didn't click on the Facebook link but I did start to take the writing of a book idea a little more seriously, starting with jotting down a few thoughts, which eventually triggered a chain reaction that had me searching for information about book publishing etc. The universe had put me on the bottom rung of a very high ladder and now it was up to me to start the climb. The universe heard what I'd wanted and gave me a way forward, it didn't give me what I wanted, only gave me a way to get it. The young man taking driving lessons will need many thousands of miles behind him before he can realise his dream of getting in that truck and I'd had many months of asking the universe for help with motivation, inspiration and vision as I began living as a writer.

For the longest time I was a karate athlete. I loved competing, I dreamt about winning individual bouts, but never about winning the championship itself. That only became important to me once I came close to the final match and it was only then that I'd wanted to go all the way. It was that lack of desire which ultimately made those achievements unattainable.

The law of attraction also works in a negative state. I've watched so many people manifesting a shit day for themselves and then feel bitter and angry about what they deemed had 'happened to them'. Phil had been involved with a lot of violence both as a kid and as an adult, he was also involved in some serious criminal activities. He had just encountered a problem with an individual that was escalating into a potential, physical kick-off and he wanted to do some regular, full-contact sparring as he planned meeting this guy for a straightener. "What the hell Is this straightener going to accomplish?" "Respect," he replied. "He needs to know not to fuck about with me." "But what if you lose?" "Well, I'll just have to train harder and then have another go."

Phil was 53 and like most people hadn't worked out that he'd been ordering the problems he was experiencing. "Phil, can you just humour me for a few minutes? When I was working the doors I'd go to bed at night thinking about violence, quite often dreaming about violence. I'd talk about the violence that I had been involved with the night before and then I would go to the gym or club and train for violence. I didn't realise it at the time but I was ordering violence, asking for it to find me and the more I ordered, the more I got. Surely there must be a different approach that you can use with this guy?" Phil eventually confessed that he didn't want violence in his life any more, his criminal days had been over a long time ago. But he was carrying around a lot of emotional baggage and his associates within that lifestyle made it very difficult for him to move on. But one day, the penny dropped so we set about replacing the order.

Instead of just getting in the ring and training for a fist fight, we went to the gym and ordered a new, fit physique. Instead of visualising punching someone in the face we visualised lifting weights to produce stronger, defined arms.

We didn't chat about violence, instead we talked about adopting a clean diet and about workout gear. We could have got in the boxing ring and had him working the pads, visualising smashing this guy's face in, but now we were running on the treadmill visualising exactly the opposite. With his own perseverance and my support, Phil was now living a life that ordered calm and peace and it wasn't that long before his order was delivered. Phil thought he needed fighting skills, but I showed him what he really needed was those people skills.

If 'Live it, become it' as a principle was so easy, everyone would be doing it. You guessed it, it's not easy and there are many obstacles and pitfalls to overcome. Phil hasn't had a clear, easy run at it. It would be a big ask for anyone to change their ordering habits overnight, but the first stage is believing that we have the power to order and receive what we really desire. I asked Phil, how many hard men, violent men, dangerous men did he know. He said he knew a lot, in fact many were close friends. My next question stunned him, or rather his own answer did. "If you know so many hard men, men who could have shown you how to really hurt your antagonist, why then did you come to me for guidance?" "I've been desiring peace and tranquillity in my life for a long time, I've always settled grievances with violence, but this time I wanted another tactic, another way of setting my life on the straight and narrow." "Phil, your thoughts, your desire was your order and the universe sent you to me."

Chapter #19

Disney

It was a blisteringly cold morning in Indianapolis, Indiana. The 'range' as it was known, registered a barometer reading of twenty below zero. The range was basically a huge yard where all the trainee truckers gathered each morning to practise the various 'big-rig' manoeuvres. We were required to do straight-line, 45 degree and 90 degree reversing drills, the wide, open, concreted space was filled with numerous learner truckers all waiting their turn for some time behind the wheel. Each student had to first pass the straight-line backing drills before they could move to the 45 then to the 90.

February in Indianapolis can get colder than something really cold and this day was even colder than that! I was standing out on the edge of the range waiting for my turn in one of only 3 trucks that were in operation. I'd enrolled with a trucking company having decided it was time for another adventure. 'Over-the-road' (OTR) trucking wasn't an occupation that had ever interested me or something I could have ever seen myself doing until now. I'd given up running the gym and really wanted to branch out, try something different. I'd often looked at these 18 wheelers and wondered, 'How the fuck do they drive those things?' Knowing that just the training itself would be a challenge and perhaps feel uncomfortable for me was actually a big part of its appeal. We're most often afraid of the things we can't do or the things that make us feel vulnerable. I saw driving a 70-foot-long tractor trailer across the length and breadth of the United States as not only scary but also a massive adventure. So there I was, about to get my truck driving licence.

When I think about it, I'm what I would call unemployable. Not because nobody would want to employ me, but because having become so intolerant of drama and bullshit, I would never be able to put up with all the crap that comes with working with groups of people. My thoughts about getting my CDL (Commercial Driver's Licence) was simply to obtain the licence, another skill in my toolkit, then I'd work out what I wanted to do with it later. I hadn't even been in a truck yet and I was already having to deal with the crap and bullshit that I have just eluded to. Sixty plus trainees, including me, were expected to stand in sub-zero conditions waiting for their turn in one of only three trucks in operation and given that each trainee was only in the truck for maybe fifteen minutes, this would mean literally hours standing in the snow, freezing my nuts off. 'I'm not doing this,' I thought as I stood so cold that I couldn't feel my feet and my face was hurting. I approached one of the instructors and handed him a piece of paper which had my mobile number written on it and a little note, 'Please text, or call me when it's my turn.' I then went inside, made myself a cup of hot chocolate, feeling so cold that I was not sure if I should drink it or throw it over my face. During my time there I made friends with a young lad, Jake, who'd followed my lead and also given the instructor his number. Jake was 35 and we'd hit it off right away. He was studying for a career in the trucking industry, following in the footsteps of his dad who had been a truck driver for many years. Jake shared that he was a recovering drug addict who'd battled with alcohol and drug abuse for many years but was now getting his shit together and securing a proper career.

As we both sat in the warm, complaining about the set up, we were approached by a manager and told that we needed to wait outside with everyone else. To be clear, this wasn't a training school that we had paid to attend. This was a company who paid trainees to obtain their licence, and in return we would work for that company for an agreed duration, so both Jake and I were essentially employees. Not for long though. I'd enrolled to learn a new skill not to be bullied by an employer, so we both quit on the spot. By this point though we'd already passed our theory tests, so we'd already earned our provisional trucker's licence, allowing us to sign up to a similar programme with a different, more employee-friendly company. "Now that's more like it, 3 trucks and only 8 trainees," Jake said as we started on our new venture. This company felt well organised and it was also a lot of fun. Instead of standing in the cold we sat in the warm cab watching and helping each other as we practised to our heart's content. Just two weeks later both Jake and I had passed our practical, road test.

I never wanted to be a trucker per-se, I just wanted the licence to expand my options but now that I'd earned it, it was time to do a little trucking. Both Jake and I were sent out on our first mission in our own trucks, each with a trainer for one week's OTR trucking. Jake headed south to the heat and sunshine of Texas, while I drew the short straw and was sent north to the ice and snow of a Canadian winter. Like I said, trucking was never going to be a long-term occupation but driving that first week, with the window down and a blue sky in front of me would probably have made it last just a little longer than it did. I'd been a fitness coach, a personal trainer, a karate instructor and many guises of the aforementioned until this point. The fitness industry was where I felt most comfortable but I knew it would benefit me to step outside my comfort zone and take on a new adventure. I frequently look for new opportunities, new projects to keep things interesting. However, sleeping in the cab's bunk bed whilst trying to block out all the sounds associated with a busy truck stop, wasn't really the adventure I was hoping for though. After a week of battling the snow and ice of an Ontario winter in a 70-foot vehicle, I was done.

Now with a commercial driver's licence in hand, doors opened for me and I began a new adventure with a vehicle delivery company which had me driving vehicles of all description throughout the USA. I delivered cars, trucks, camper vans and even those big yellow school buses to cities like Chicago, New Orleans and Kansas. One day I'd be driving through the Smoky mountains of Tennessee, the next I was waking up just a few miles from the White House in Washington DC; places the average Coventry kid could only dream about visiting. Boy, was I having an adventure in all corners of the US!

Prior to delivering vehicles though I'd taken on a different adventure - Orlando, Florida; 'if you can dream it, you can do it.' Figment, my son's favourite cuddly toy, sang a song called Imagination and after I'd quit the big rigs I'd imagined how much fun it would be to drive Disney coaches in the sunshine state. I had my CDL, so why not? All I needed to do was obtain passenger endorsements on my licence which enabled me to drive passenger vehicles. Another skill? Yeah, let's do this. During my time in Orlando, I drove the Disney Magical Express which collected passengers from the airport and transported them to all the Disney resorts. I also drove the Disney Cruise line coach to and from Cape Canaveral, about an hour out of Orlando. How many Coventry kids can say they have done that?

I was working for a company who was contracted by Disney, so other driving duties were also involved. The iTrolley is a vehicle that transports passengers along International Drive. Everyone who's visited Orlando will know what I am talking about. It's a pretty cool looking vehicle, tram-like (without the tracks), green in colour with attractive advertisements adorning most of the exterior. The front end displayed a somewhat sculpted cartoon face, think Thomas the Tank Engine! Once inside, passengers listen to music while sitting on what resembles wooden park benches. As cool and fun as this vehicle looked, it was a bus and I was the driver who hadn't counted on having to stop at bus stops, take fares and put up with all the shit that comes with that job. I loved the weather and the lifestyle in Florida and had an expectation that this was going to be my permanent home, but not at the cost of my happiness.

I'd also done some shifts running coaches to and from the Orlando theme parks, transporting tourists between their hotel and the world-famous Disney parks. I was learning the ropes, in particular, where all the pick-ups and drop-offs were situated at each park so I had an instructor on board shadowing me.

One particular day I was driving along a very busy intersection. I'd checked my mirrors, indicated and changed lanes. I then suddenly heard a car horn followed by someone shouting at the top of their voice. The instructor asked me to stop straight away. We got out of the coach to see a guy walking towards the front of the coach, claiming that I had hit his yellow taxi cab. Of course, I hadn't, there was zero impact! On inspecting the front of his cab, we saw there was a dent, but given its location there was no way it had been caused by the coach and there was nothing on his cab to indicate it was us. It suddenly hit me, he was looking for some kind of compensation, saying that I was at fault! These incidents weren't uncommon but regardless, I was expected to report the incident (what incident?) to the safety manager and not leave the scene until the police had arrived. "Ok, let's wait for the police but I'm not taking responsibility for something I haven't done." Back on the coach the instructor called my supervisor, something that was protocol after an accident, whilst we remained parked up, traffic speeding around us. I went back outside to the taxi driver, "The police are on their way." Lo and behold! Speedy Gonzales jumped in his cab and was gone. Arriba! Arriba! I went back onto the coach, "It's all good, the taxi guy has gone." "Did you get the cab driver's name, ID, number?" Of course, I hadn't.

With the coach still blocking traffic, we sat waiting for a supervisor to arrive. "So does this shit happen a lot then?" I asked. "Enough," came the reply, "but it's keeping Disney sweet that is the hardest thing, that's why there is such a big turnover with drivers." He didn't give me any specifics, but it was clear that this job had the potential to be super stressful. I'd decided long before the supervisor arrived that I was going to walk. This is the thing that happens when you genuinely don't care what people think, you do what you feel is best for you. The supervisor arrived and immediately started to read me the riot act. "Wait, wait, let me stop you right there. Do I drive the coach back to the yard or does somebody else want to do it, 'cos I'm done?" Kids bully other kids when they know so they have something over them. Employers bully employees for the same reason. I didn't need, want, or care about this job. I had nothing to lose and having nothing to lose puts you in a very powerful position.

A few months later I was back in Indianapolis, with Disney coaches a distant memory. I get a call from Jake, asking if I'm able to do him a favour and give him a ride to Gas City.

He explains that his girlfriend's ex-boyfriend had shot her in the face, he wanted to help. Err what?! She was in hospital and he didn't know what condition she was in. Of course I raced to pick Jake up and we headed the 70 miles north to where he said the ambulance had taken her to. Knowing we were driving to a situation which could have turned violent at any moment, Jake asked, "Can you take me to my house first, I need to pick up my gun." "Hold on, there, my friend, I think you need to start over, you've now put me in a very difficult position!" I pulled the car over and looked at Jake, hoping he'd be able to see what I was thinking. "Jake, I'm not taking you to pick up a gun!" "Oh no, I just wanted to make sure I was armed in case the boyfriend showed up, that's all, I wasn't going to do anything." I drove directly to the hospital and dropped Jake off. As it turned out, Jake's girlfriend had shot herself in the face in a suicide attempt that had gone wrong, thankfully she survived. Jake sadly died of heroin overdose just a few months later.

As I reflect on the many places that I have visited, the people I've met and the adventures I've had, one thing sticks out as true - everyone is in their own battle. It doesn't matter what their social status, their wealth, or their geographical location, we're all constantly fighting a battle with ourselves

Chapter #20

The Author

The very fact that you are reading this means that I am a published author, that's crazy! Just like you, there are some things that I would never ever have believed about myself. I'm not a writer, maybe after reading this book some of you are saying, yes you are right, you are not a writer. However I'm now a published author. This is my book and I wrote every word of it. When I say wrote, what I really mean is, well mostly dictated. Let me explain. It had been mentioned to me on so many occasions that I should write a book, I never once took the suggestion seriously though; writing isn't what I do, or what I've enjoyed in the past. I don't even write letters so a book would be totally out of the question. That said, I have written quite a few columns for a martial arts magazine, so writing content which is interesting and often informative to me, isn't alien. I have, however, struggled with keeping to a strict schedule. The magazines I wrote for understandably wanted the column content to be ready on their calendar, not mine. They had deadlines to meet so I was expected to submit my work on time, every time, which I did.

When I first started writing for the magazine it was exciting, but the excitement quickly turned to dread when I discovered that inspiration doesn't just happen when you want it to. I had to produce a new article every month. Staying motivated enough to sit down and write proved to be a problem. Looking back now, it's clear that the options to write, the process itself, was fairly limited. Using a desktop computer meant I had to go into the room where the computer was located, think creatively and have the discipline to keep going, even when the inspiration waned and there was nothing in my head. I found that I often wasn't in the mood. This was a discipline that frustratingly I didn't have. I knew that writing for the magazine would help my career, increase my profile within the karate world, so although it was uncomfortable for me I knew I had to do it. I reached out to other columnists for advice but the advice they gave wasn't what I wanted to hear. Many of them completed a year's worth of columns (articles) over just a few weeks of writing, so they had all of their work pretty much stockpiled and ready to go, occasionally only having to edit work that was already done. I, on the other hand, had to force myself into the room where the computer was, having procrastinated right up to just a few days before the article was due.

When it came to writing this book however, everything had changed. Technology is such now that anybody can literally write a book, publish a book, and sell the book without ever leaving their house. Those days of having to find a quiet, tranquil space to begin writing have long gone. That's not to say that many writers still do prefer that method though. The first few months of writing, for me, can only be described as torture as I soon fell back into the mindset of the columnist who had struggled to meet those deadlines. Having committed to making this book a reality I initially thought that a quiet, tranquil environment, a room where there would be no disruptions, a place to set up my laptop would be ideal. I sort of pictured myself as Johnny Depp in the movie, Secret Window. My first attempt in that set up just didn't feel right, though, and I couldn't understand why.

I remember just sitting, staring at my laptop. Where the hell do I start? What format do I write in? Do I open a Word document, or is there book writing software that I should be using? How do I save everything I've written with confidence so I know it'll be there when I log back in tomorrow? What if I write some really good stuff and then I lose it all? Should I print as I go and save a hard copy? I had so many questions and no real answers so understandably it didn't take me very long before I began to lose interest in the whole project altogether. As I've said, I'm not a writer. I don't know about chapter headings, subheadings (are they even a thing, I'm sure I've seen that written down somewhere?!) I didn't know how many chapters I wanted to write, how many words the book should have and I didn't even have a book title. I knew what I wanted to write about but I just couldn't get anything out of my head and into any kind of written form. I forced myself to sit down and produce a basic, draft first chapter. It didn't even resemble anything that I felt comfortable sharing with anyone initially and it had taken me a week to write less than 2,000 words. I had been using the hunt and peck method as it's referred to when typing - basically hunting down each letter I wanted, then pecking it with my index finger. Not only is this method painstakingly slow but it also had me losing my train of thought and soon enough I was staring at a document that was just a jumble of words that didn't really make a lot of sense.

There must be a more productive way, surely? It wasn't too long before I sent a text message to a friend and it hit me. I don't type messages, I speak them. If I can talk to the phone, and it types the words for me, surely I can do the same with anything I'm writing? After a little research I discovered that indeed, I didn't have to sit down in one location, set up a laptop and be a slave to the project. I also discovered that I didn't need to worry too much about spelling, grammar, and punctuation etc. I already had the software in my hand that would correct that all for me, all I had to do was just press the small microphone button on the phone and talk. This discovery was mind-blowing, how didn't I know about this already? You have to be shitting me?! I own a book writing tool, I can take it anywhere, in the car, on the bus, train, airplane, or the top of a mountain if I so desired and the best part, if you haven't heard the best part already, it's totally free! As I sit writing, or should I say dictating right now, I have the entire manuscript, the whole book, every chapter on this phone. All I have to do is open a chapter to amend or edit. That's right. I am currently sitting in a comfortable armchair with a cup of coffee, music playing while I'm writing this chapter. My phone is Bluetooth to a printer so all I have to do for a hard copy is press 'print'.

Once I discovered how this all worked, I scrapped everything that I'd already written and I started over. The first thing I did was to write a complete draft chapter. It gave me great comfort knowing that the only person that was ever going to see this draft was me. I would just talk to the phone and watch the phone type. If the phone picked up the word incorrectly, I would simply go in by hand and correct that word. This all looked far too easy; there has to be a catch! Nope, no catch. There's always a way, you just have to look for it. Having overcome the difficulty of how to get the words out and into written form, I thought I would now be in for an easy ride. How wrong I was! As the weeks went on, the questions of self-doubt popped into my head, 'Who am I writing for, is what I am writing even worth reading? What if I'm delusional, what if nobody is going to be interested in this book?'

The list of negative thoughts can be overwhelming. Whole chapters completed, only to then be totally deleted. I had gone down a rabbit hole and all I could hear screaming from the pages was me ranting and getting personal shit off my chest. Writing a book of this nature is indeed very cathartic. It has forced me to open doors that I had closed and assumed were locked forever. Everyone knows how a song you've not heard in a decade can stir up memories. Some happy, some sad and some that, well, let's not even go there.

The writing itself was no longer a problem but staying motivated and believing in myself was a daily, often hourly struggle. The kid who ran out of the classroom, embarrassed because he couldn't spell a word was now writing a book, how the fuck did that happen? 'I am an author'. I have probably said those words thousands of times now and have reached the point where if I'm asked, "So what do you do?" I now respond with 'author' because 'I am' with self-belief and conviction is how you become who you want to be and how I achieved the things I had.

My perception is my reality; change my perception, change my reality. You have read this phrase numerous times now but it's worth mentioning again and again because everything I am, everything you are, starts with your own perception. I am reminded here about the story I read in a book called Psycho Cybernetics. A travelling salesman was given his own patch, his own area to build customers. After a short time, he had built his customer base that brought in sales of £3,000 per day. His bosses were extremely pleased with him and quickly moved him to another far more affluent area. After a short period of time once again he built a customer base that brought in sales of £3,000 per day. His bosses were confused, he was a superb salesman. The very upmarket, affluent area he was now in charge of should be bringing in at least three times the revenue of his previous area. The bosses decided to move him once again but no matter what area he was assigned to, he always produced sales of £3,000. On speaking to the salesman it became clear that he was extremely happy with his lifestyle, his house, his car and basically his financial situation. The commission he received from £3,000 in sales a day was more than enough for him. The company perceived him as a high flyer, a salesman who could easily make himself a millionaire; he perceived himself as a family man who did what was required to put food on the table and a roof over his family's head. He was, is and always would be a £3,000 per day salesman.

Just like him I'd put limits on myself, not necessarily financial ones but rather ones based on a lack of confidence. The biggest take away I wanted people to get from this book was the realisation that 'there is always a way' . There are many roads that lead to the same destination and it's a personal choice which road you choose. There was simply no way I could have written this book if I'd travelled the road that many authors take. I found the road that worked best for me and now I have reached my destination I can come here again as I am now confident about the journey. My hope is that having read my story, you too can chase your dreams and figure out your own way of getting where you want to go. The only limits we have are the ones we place on ourselves.

Ingram Content Group UK Ltd.
Milton Keynes UK
UKHW010630140723
425136UK00001B/21

9 781915 796783